THE HISTORY OF COSTA RICA

BRIEF, UP-TO-DATE AND ILLUSTRATED

Iván Molina
Steven Palmer

EDITORIAL DE LA UNIVERSIDAD DE COSTA RICA

972.86
M722h Molina Jiménez, Iván, 1961-
The history of Costa Rica : brief, up-to-date and illustrated / Iván Molina, Steven Palmer. – 1. ed., 5a. reimpr. – San José, C.R. : Editorial Universidad de Costa Rica, 2006.
174 p. : il., mapas.

ISBN 9977-67-468-X

1. COSTA RICA – HISTORIA. I. Palmer, Steven, 1961- coautor. II. Título.

CIP/1372
CC/SIBDI.UCR

Edition approved by Comisión Editorial de la Universidad de Costa Rica
First edition: 1998
Fifth reprinted: 2006

Cover desing: *Juan Carlos Fallas Z.*

Apdo. 75-2060 • Tel.: 207 5310 • Fax: 207 5257 • E-mail: editucr@cariari.ucr.ac.cr •
Página web: www.editorial.ucr.ac.cr

CONTENTS

PROLOGUE

AN EXCURSION TO THE PAST

This brief history, the first of its kind in the English language, offers readers from all parts of the world a condensed and illustrated account of Costa Rica's past. Its pages focus on the principal events and patterns in the country's colorful and exceptional history. The story begins in ancient times when the tropical forests hid the elusive footsteps of primitive hunters, and brings us to the ever more urban and complex present. The sweep is wide, ranging from the domestication of plants between 4,000 and 1,000 B.C., to the Civil War of 1948, and from the rise of the coffee and banana industries in the nineteenth century to the tourism boom of the 1990s.

Travellers.

The book is not a publicity pamphlet promoting Costa Rica's natural wonders to tourists. Instead, this slim volume invites the reader to get to know the essential background and characteristics of the country they are living in or visiting. In some ways the invitation is similar to those extended every day by travel agencies and tour companies, but in this case the excursion is not to a volcano, to a beach, or to an island – this tour is a journey into the past.

Sign on and you will head out on safari with primitive hunters, observe the everyday labors of the tribal societies of the sixteenth century, and participate in the Conquest. You will sojourn through colonial villages, experience the expansion of coffee farming after 1830, and witness the boom of banana cultivation in the virgin jungles of the late nineteenth century. And, as the tour brings us back to our point of departure, you will watch a nation take shape and a democracy take root, participate in the protests of peasants, artisans and workers, and get a close-up look at the crisis of 1930 and the conflict of 1948. Finally, you will visit the ruins of Costa Rica's social democratic dream (1950-1978), and enjoy an afternoon of shopping in the malls of a neoliberal and thoroughly modern tropical republic.

Fasten your seatbelt –some turbulence is expected– and have a pleasant flight.

In January [1915], *the time had come to leave San José and go to Nicaragua... As I look back, however, I think that my stay in Costa Rica was in some ways the pleasantest part of my Central American experience, though not the most interesting. There was no other country where I felt that I was participating so fully in the social life of the community, and none where I found people more attractive and more friendly.*

Dana Gardner Munro, US scholar and diplomat.

CHAPTER 1

TRAILS OF THE FIRST PEOPLES (12,000 B.C.-1500 A.D.)

Bands of primitive people who specialized in hunting began to occupy America about forty thousand years ago. The immigrants came from Asia, crossing the Bering Straits and occupying the north-western part of the continent. Gradually, over a period of thousands of years, they moved southwards. The everyday life of these small, nomadic bands of close kin was taken up by hunting, gathering and fishing in rivers, lakes and oceans. They knew nothing about growing foodstuffs, and their division of labor scarcely went beyond criteria of age and sex.

Arrowheads. Turrialba, 12,000-8,000 B.C.

The territory that is now Costa Rica was likely occupied between 12,000 and 8,000 B.C. The early settlers inhabited a landscape dominated by tropical forests. Some of the animals they hunted became extinct a long time ago: mastodons, giant sloths, horses and camel-like creatures. Their tools were made from stone (especially silica), wood, hides and bones. By and large, these objects were designed for hunting: a variety of pointed projectiles, hammers, scrapers, knives and chisels, for example.

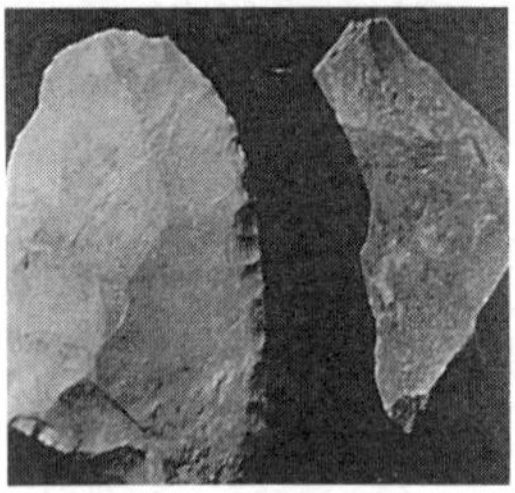

Scraping instruments. Turrialba, 12,000-8,000 B.C.

Between 8,000 and 4,000 B.C., these early inhabitants tended to become sedentary. Either by accident, or by picking up knowledge from neighboring groups, they learned to domesticate plants. Archaeologists have found evidence that settlements were increasingly made up of more people and had greater permanence. At the same time, in the course of repeated gathering in the same forests, these primitive peoples acquired experience that allowed a gradual selection of certain varieties of plants and animals for human consumption.

The transition to farming was a slow process that extended between 4,000 and 1,000 years before Christ. Costa Rica's position on the isthmus made it a meeting place of North and South American cultural currents. This allowed the inhabitants to acquire knowledge about the domestication of root vegetables like yucca and sweet potato common in the tropical areas of South America, as well as to learn about the growing of grains like corn, more typical of the semi-arid zones of Mexico. The influence was itself geographically marked: on the Caribbean side, where contact with South America was common, the cultivation of tubers predominated; corn and beans were prevalent in the Central Valley and on the Pacific lowlands, areas that related more with the north.

Hunting turtles.

With the domestication of agriculture came changes in the instruments of labor. Grinding and nut-cracking stones, as well as other tools for processing vegetables, were supplemented by objects for better exploiting the forests, such as axes, hatchets and levers. The use of a variety of organic products (wood, teeth, shells and bamboo) also intensified, at the same time that pottery for preparing and storing food became more sophisticated. The typical product of the potter's skill was the *tecomate,* a large vessel with a narrow mouth used for storing foodstuffs.

Between 1,000 B.C. and 800 A.D., the early societies underwent decisive changes. The principal one was the consolidation of agriculture, which gathered momentum at the expense of the most basic survival activities (hunting, fishing and gathering). Notable at first was the planting of root vegetables, yucca being the most common, which was associated with the creation of more specialized artifacts such as *budares,* large ceramic dishes used to cook the root. The cultivation of corn, at first simply one among many agricultural activities, successfully expanded in the five hundred years before Christ.

Figure on a *metate* (used for preparing food). Pacific north, 500-800 A.D.

At the same time that they permitted population growth, advances in the production of foodstuffs reinforced sedentary habits. This in turn was the basis of growing knowledge that came from the daily observation of flora and fauna as they were being domesticated. Permanence stimulated the diversification of crafts, and artisans began to dedicate themselves to fashioning objects beyond those necessary for survival: necklaces, *metates* (flat stones for grinding with elaborately sculpted bases), multi-colored ceramics and ocarinas. Sedentary living also demanded that a greater amount of territory be accessible so that cultivation might be rotated as soils were depleted.

Social and political organization changed alongside the transformation of production methods. The basic change was the passage from the small band, dedicated to hunting and gathering, to the tribe. The tribe had a greater populace, it specialized in agriculture and it inhabited a defined territory. Essentially, as a village subdivided on the basis of population growth, it gave origin to other village units, with which it would generally unite in a confederation. Kinship networks were the axis of this complex and intermittent process.

The egalitarian character of the first villages disappeared as the division of labor increased, and as a hierarchy of villages took shape. Aside from promoting demographic growth, the production of an agricultural surplus promoted the rise of specialized roles, such as administrators for organizing the distribution of the bounty of the land, and warriors for defending the territory. Equally important were the functions linked to the cult of the ancestors and other religious activities. During the first 500 years after Christ, a social hierarchy grew, with the figure of the *cacique* (or chief) at the top, and power and wealth became concentrated in certain settlements.

Figure of a shaman. Atlantic area, 500-1000 A.D.

The links between villages of unequal importance, which together marked off a specific territory, were the basis of the *cacicazgos* (chieftainships). These early political associations were also the basis of commerce, which involved some surprisingly long-distance trade. The settlers of the Caribbean side of the country were part of the mercantile circuits of their neighbors in Panama, Colombia and Ecuador.

Indigenous vessel.

In Nicoya, the northern influence of Mesoamerican (Mexican and Central American) indigenous groups was more prominent. The groups of Costa Rica's Central Valley benefitted from the influence of both poles. The merchandise coming from Costa Rican territory was not of great importance to this extensive network of exchange; it was essentially confined to perishable articles like salt, cocoa beans, quetzal feathers and dyes made from crushed shells. Mesoamerican traditions lost strength between 500 and 800 A.D.

Southern cultures took advantage of this to broaden their influence throughout Costa Rican territory. The change was most clearly registered in craftwork. Jade sculpting, which had followed Mayan models, was displaced by the working of metals, especially gold. In the lovely gold jewelry and adornments for warrior garb one can see shapes and styles similar to those found in Panama and Colombia. The available evidence, although fragmentary, confirms that Chibcha civilization had an enormous influence over the first peoples of Costa Rica.

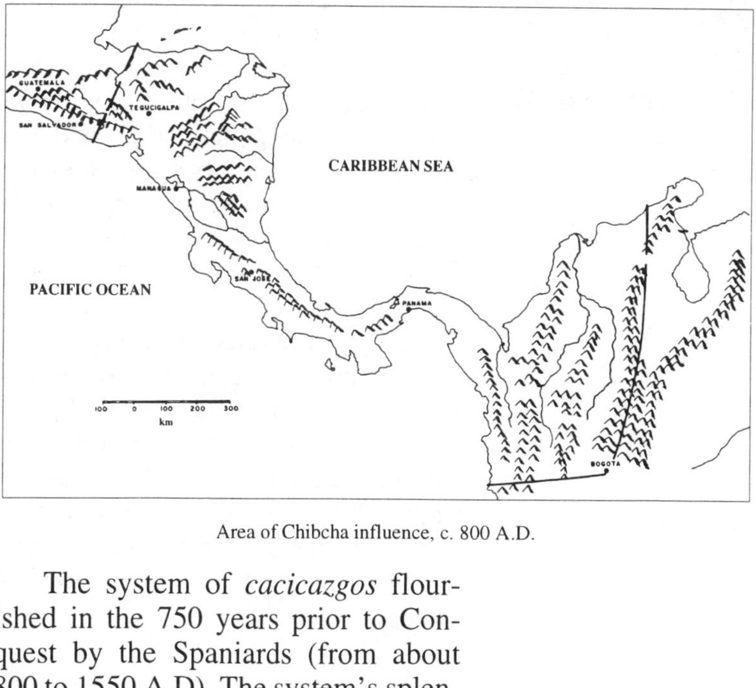

Area of Chibcha influence, c. 800 A.D.

The system of *cacicazgos* flourished in the 750 years prior to Conquest by the Spaniards (from about 800 to 1550 A.D). The system's splendor came from a more intensive production of grains and roots, which combined the use of natural fertilizers and irrigation with the slashing and burning of the forests to prepare fields for agriculture. Farming was complemented by hunting and fishing, and by the gathering of salt, fruits, beeswax and honey. A more diverse set of artisanal activities was needed for the growth of the principal settlements, which began to acquire aqueducts, roads, bridges, houses, temples and palisades for defense.

Warrior with axe and head. Atlantic area, 500-1000 A.D.

As *cacicazgos* became larger, social differentiation increased. Inevitably, a military and religious nobility was consolidated. The nobles ruled over workers and slaves, these latter usually prisoners captured in tribal conflicts. Kinship networks and the principle of reciprocity (fair exchange of goods among equals) were outweighed by this political hierarchy, which allowed shamans and warriors to exploit their social inferiors. Charged with regulating everyday life, these groups arranged the distribution of riches, power and knowledge in their favor. This model of domination was well established by the sixteenth century when tribal societies had to face rivals far different from any enemy they might have known to that point.

CHAPTER 2

CACICAZGOS AND *SEÑORÍOS* (1500-1570)

On the eve of the Spanish Conquest of Costa Rica, diverse indigenous societies were dispersed throughout south-eastern Central America. They were politically fragmented, and neither their social organization nor their use of technology was sophisticated in comparison with the better known Mayan indigenous groups of northern Central America.

Indigenous people in the forest.

The civilizations of the Guatemalan and Salvadoran highlands, and of the lowlands of the Yucatan peninsula and the Gulf of Honduras, had large and dense populations, and displayed great cultural diversity. For the most part Mayan, by the sixteenth century these peoples had become strongly influenced by Mexican cultures. The ruins of the Mayan cities are spectacular records of the urban growth, the architectural techniques, the precise knowledge of astronomy and the artistic vision that graced this civilization. Mayan, and later Aztec, influence was felt far to the south, and shaped some elements of Costa Rica's pre-Columbian cultures.

At the beginning of the sixteenth century about 400,000 indigenous people lived in the territory that would become Costa Rica. The majority of them were located in the Pacific northwest and in the Central Valley. The population growth that had come with more intensive agriculture (that of corn in particular) did not lead to any drastic transformation of the landscape. The aboriginal peoples made room for themselves in a lush tropical wilderness, characterized by impenetrable forests, vigorous rivers, daunting swamps, exuberant vegetation, dense mountain ranges and animal life that was diverse and often savage.

The roughest mountains I have ever seen and, in the opinion of some, the roughest that have ever been seen. Intolerable conditions of hunger and thirst slowed our attempts to slice open narrow pathways, and to climb and descend great peaks, so cavernous and drenched in rain that the sight of the sun was a marvel.

Juan Vázquez de Coronado, one of the conquistadors of Costa Rica, 1563.

The village was the basis of indigenous civilization. It was the axis of everyday life, which was taken up by agriculture, crafts, commerce and war. Once conjoined in a federation, the villages became local cells of a *cacicazgo,* or chieftainship. The place each *cacicazgo* occupied in the hierarchy of regional political power varied according to the size of its population and of the territory under its control. Beyond this, a *cacicazgo* could integrate itself into a larger, more centralized political and military unit called a *señorío,* a kind of fiefdom with jurisdiction over a vast and disputed territory.

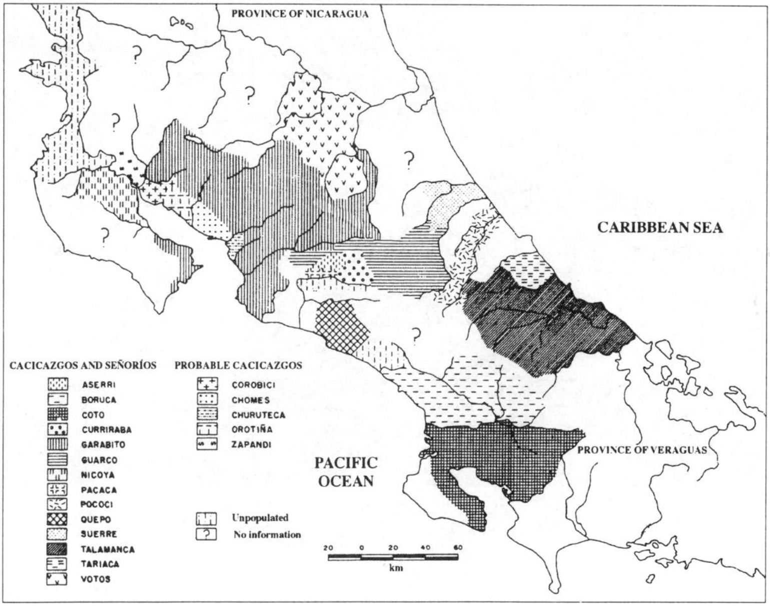

Cacicazgos and *Señoríos* of Costa Rica, 16th century.

On the eve of Conquest, the *cacicazgo* of Nicoya was the most important in Costa Rica's Pacific north. Other principal chieftainships were the Votos of the San Carlos plains, near the present border with Nicaragua; the Suerre, Pococí, Tariaca and Talamanca of the Caribbean lowlands; the Quepo, Coto and Boruca of the Pacific south; and the *señoríos* of Guarco and Garabito in the Central Valley. Guarco territory was concentrated to the east of present-day Cartago, though it also included areas between Alajuela and San José. The domains of the Garabito extended from Esparza to the banks of the San Juan River.

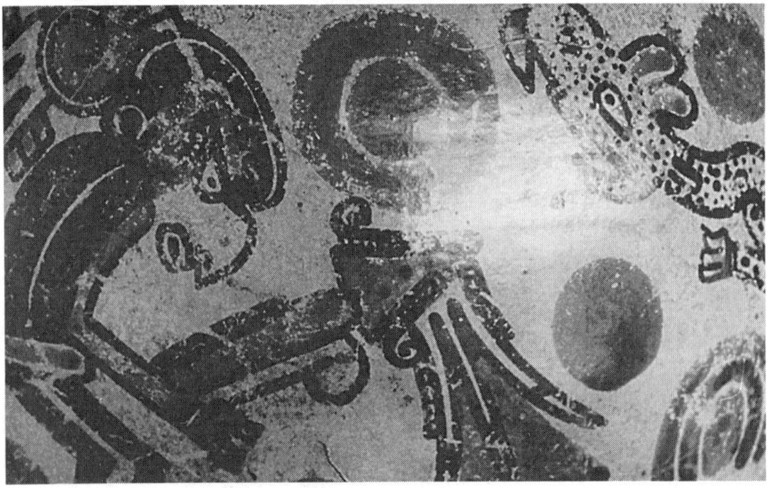

Sacred struggle between light and darkness (detail).
Pacific north, 800-1350 A.D.

An indigenous nobility ruled over these different types of territorial organizations. At the top of the largest political entities were lords, while lesser federations were ruled by principal and secondary *caciques.* The nobility was united by kinship ties, and its authority was enhanced by claims to special religious and magical powers. These noble leaders fulfilled particular roles with regard to warfare, commerce and relations with supernatural beings. In doing so, they consolidated privileged positions that allowed them to exploit their social inferiors, and to gain access to gold and slaves. Political power was inherited through matrilineal succession, and the origins of that power were associated with venerable ancestors, a mythical weight that increased the respect for noble lineage.

Indigenous dwelling in Sipurio, Talamanca. Oil on canvas. Luis Sanclemente, 1892.

There were notable cultural differences among the many indigenous groups of Costa Rica. Architecturally, the elliptical house prevailed in the Pacific north, while a circular dwelling was common in the Central Valley. In marked contrast to these, the typical construction of the Caribbean side and in the Pacific south was the *palenque,* a kind of longhouse protected by stockades and capable of housing 300 to 400 people. The linguistic terrain was also varied. Since oral communication predominated, the small region had a large number of languages. It is likely, however, that Huetar, the language used by the *señoríos* of Garabito and Guarco, had become a lingua franca for many other tribes.

The religion of the indigenous groups was animist. They believed that people, animals and natural phenomena all had spirits, and that these spirits could be bad, damaging or dangerous. Funeral rites displayed expectations of immortality. Special treatment was given to the corpse, particularly when it belonged to a member of the nobility. The dead were buried with different objects (sometimes even gold objects), and with their slaves who were sacrificed for the occasion so that they might continue serving their master or mistress in the next life.

The Tuarco chief [was with]... *an Indian wrapped in blankets, with gold and other things, above a barbecue... More than sixty Indian men and many Indian women were wailing according to their funeral custom. It made me sad to think that four days earlier they had killed four or six boys in order to bury them along with the dead chief.*

Juan Vázquez de Coronado, 1563.

Religious activities took place in temples, similar to the dwellings but smaller in size. These sacred places also served to house ritual objects: musical instruments, masks and mats. They were the site of ceremonies where priests professed the cults of certain icons (which were made of gold, to judge by the way the Spanish sacked these temples). The shaman fulfilled various crucial functions: he answered the queries of the community, foretold the future, and served as intermediary between the supernatural realm and that of everyday life.

In the sixteenth century, human sacrifice and cannibalism were practiced in Costa Rica's Pacific north. The *cacicazgo* of Nicoya organized such ritual celebrations three times a year, coinciding with the corn harvests. On the day of the festival, with the nobility dressed in full regalia and painted for the occasion, a ceremonial mixture of alcohol –*chicha*– was drunk, and expressives dances were performed before the temple. Then five or six people of either sex, previously selected, were brought to the altar at the top of the temple, their hearts cut out, their heads chopped off, and their bodies rolled down the side of the temple so that their flesh could be consumed with all the solemnity of the moment.

Human sacrifice during funeral rites or harvest ceremonies was directly related to the military sphere, since warfare was the principal source of the slaves. War was constant and widespread. Sometimes groups went to war to defend or to expand their territory. They might also fight to gain or maintain access to important trade routes, or to acquire gold through pillage. Other times, wars were fought to impose –or to oppose– patterns of unequal exchange, or they resulted from a scarcity of food or materials that might occur after natural disasters or political conflicts. War was also undertaken to steal adults and children. Prisoners added to the labor force, and women of fertile age gave the tribes of

They take a woman or man... and lead him up the mount and open up his side and extract his heart, and the first blood is sacrificed to the sun. Then they decapitate the man along with four or five others on a stone... and they throw the corpses over the side to roll down, where they are collected and subsequently eaten as sacred and valued food.

Gonzalo Fernández de Oviedo, 1527.

their captors greater possibilities for population growth.

War also had a variety of magical dimensions. Robbing the gold of a rival band weakened them, for example, and enemies were decapitated and their severed heads used as trophies. The arms employed in warfare were bows, arrows, spears, stones and shields made of wood or of hides. Among the battle tactics were ambushes, the use of traps, surprise attacks, plunder, and the burning of crops and villages. Military success depended on the alliances that could be forged between the contenders and their neighbors. This was a traditional strategy that was extremely useful for the Spanish during the Conquest.

The end of one civilization and the beginning of another.

CHAPTER 3

CONQUEST AND RESISTANCE (1502-1570)

The Spanish subjugation of Costa Rica came late in the conquest of America, and it was never really completed. The conquistadors were actually preceded by the arrival of their viruses and bacteria, which began to decimate the indigenous populations. Though the Costa Rican education system has propagated the myth that there were virtually no indigenous people in the territory when the Spanish arrived, in fact there were approximately 400,000 – a figure that would not be matched by the Hispanic, mestizo populace of Costa Rica until the 1920s. By 1569, once the Spaniards had managed to gain a permanent foothold, there were only 120,000 indigenous people, and by 1611 there were a mere 10,000 left.

Indigenous resistance.

The most damage to the native people was wrought by epidemic diseases caused by contact with invaders from another continent. The immune systems of the indigenous groups were incapable of dealing with new viruses like smallpox, typhus, whooping cough, measles and influenza. This human catastrophe was exacerbated by warfare and the horrific exploitation of indigenous labor.

Much of Central America was conquered between 1519 and 1523. There were two converging waves: one moving south from Mexico and another heading north from Panama. The fact that Central America's indigenous groups were so politically fragmented made Spanish control extremely difficult. Spanish efforts to consolidate their power were further complicated by endless conflicts among the invaders themselves. This political chaos was the backdrop to the region's first economic "boom" between 1536 and 1540 which was based on the genocidal enslavement of the indigenous groups of Nicoya and Nicaragua, exported in huge numbers to the Antilles, the Gulf of Honduras, Peru and Panama.

In one single ship that was carrying [to Peru?] *four hundred Indian men and women* [slaves], *not fifty were left by the end of the voyage, for the rest had all expired.*

Act prohibiting the export of indigenous people from Nicaragua and Nicoya, 1536.

The political organization of Central America was stabilized between 1540 and 1570. In 1548, the *Audiencia* of Santiago de Guatemala was founded, and from 1570 onwards it had jurisdiction over all the territory stretching between Chiapas (currently on the Mexican side of the border with Guatemala) and the southern frontier region of Costa Rica (which was itself divided into two jurisdictions, the Province of Costa Rica and the Corregimiento of Nicoya). The Kingdom of Guatemala, as it was also known, was an administrative entity that had a great deal of autonomy from the powerful Viceroyalty of New Spain (Mexico), and the region was able to preserve that separate status throughout the colonial period.

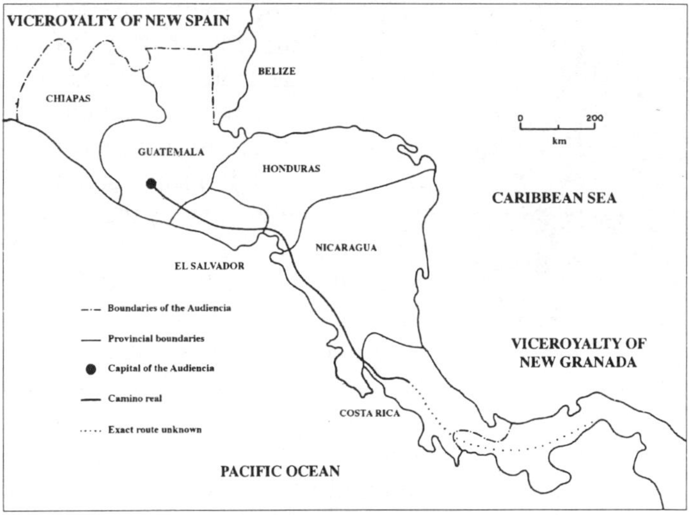

Audiencia of Guatemala, c. 1800.

Civil and ecclesiastical officials exercised the greatest authority within this new institutional framework. They were most in control in the highlands, and on the piedmont and coastal plains of the Pacific side of the isthmus. The Caribbean side remained virtually unconquered, given its distance from the main population centers, its uncomfortable climate and the tenacious resistance of its indigenous groups.

The conquest of Costa Rica was late by regional standards. Its initial phase was part of the Spanish effort to subdue the Pacific side of Central America. In 1519, Hernán Ponce de León reached the Gulf of Nicoya, but he did not disembark; in 1522, Gil González Dávila explored the area by land and traded with the indigenous groups; and in 1524, Francisco Fernández de Córdoba founded Villa Bruselas. This first settlement of the Spanish invaders on Costa Rican soil was short-lived. It disappeared in 1527, due to disputes among the conquistadors and aboriginal attacks which forced the last settlers to abandon the site.

Exploration of Costa Rican Pacific coast.

Although the town had a short life, its foundation inaugurated a violent dismantling of the *cacicazgos* of the Pacific north-west. Apart from being exported as slaves, indigenous people were distributed among the conquerors in *encomienda,* a kind of serfdom that obliged native people to provide labor and goods to their *encomendero.* The local indigenous nobility often collaborated with the conquistadors. This limited the possibilities for concerted armed resistance by Costa Rica's first peoples, who sometimes opted for flight into the mountainous forests. Another image of the devastating effect of the Spanish invasion can be grasped by figures from Nicoya that show a drop in the number of men of working age from 2,000 in 1529 to 500 in 1557.

On the Caribbean side of the territory, the conquest was even more violent – and even less successful. Columbus landed in Limón in 1502, but the first, disastrous exploration of the coast was carried out in 1510 by Diego de Nicuesa. His early example was imitated twenty years later by Felipe Gutiérrez (1534-1535), and subsequently by Hernán Sánchez de Badajoz (1539-1541), Rodrigo de Contreras (1540-1541) and Diego Gutiérrez (1542). The aboriginals, friendly at first, began to offer military resistance to the invaders once the Spanish started to demand food and gold.

I arrived in the land of Cariay [in 1502], *where I stopped to mend and provision the ships, and to give some rest to the crew members who were quite ill... There I heard tales of the gold mines in the province of Ciamba that I was searching for.*

Christopher Columbus, letter written in Jamaica, July 1503.

In their desire to subdue the people on the Caribbean coast, the conquistadors founded Villa de la Concepción in 1535, and Badajoz and Marbella in 1540, amongst other settlements. All were ephemeral. The failure of these efforts was due to conflicts among the Spaniards, difficult terrain, an incapacity to endure the climate, the complexity of receiving supplies from other parts of the isthmus and fierce indigenous resistance. This violent resistance was a result of the Spaniards' tendency to mistreat rather than to co-opt the hierarchy of chiefs. More dispersed and fragmented than their counterparts in the Pacific north, the native people also enjoyed the cover of the thick forests, and they did not hesitate to pull up their crops in order to make the invading forces withdraw for lack of food.

Whipping and dismemberment of indigenous people.

The death of Diego Gutiérrez at the hands of the indigenous people was the beginning of a long hiatus in the process of conquest in this part of the country. The next attempt to conquer the Caribbean side began in 1560, when the cleric Juan de Estrada Rávago left Granada, Nicaragua, and reached Bocas del Toro (on the present-day border with Panama), where he founded the town of Castillo de Austria. The settlement was moved to the mouth of the Suerre River due to scarcity of food and strong indigenous opposition. It was abandoned soon afterward. A number of subsequent expeditions organized in the seventeenth century met similar fates.

The Central Valley was not conquered easily either. The first expedition to penetrate the territory was that of Juan de Cavallón in 1561, which resulted in the foundation of the town of Garcimuñoz, a settlement called Los Reyes and a port called Landecho. All these footholds, however, were extremely precarious due to opposition from the indigenous groups. The real conqueror of the Central Valley was Juan Vásquez de Coronado, who after 1563 embarked on a mission to co-opt the *caciques* and lords. Oriented by this objective, the invading party explored the territory in detail and made efforts to forge alliances with different indigenous groups. In the process, Vázquez de Coronado founded Cartago, Costa Rica's colonial capital.

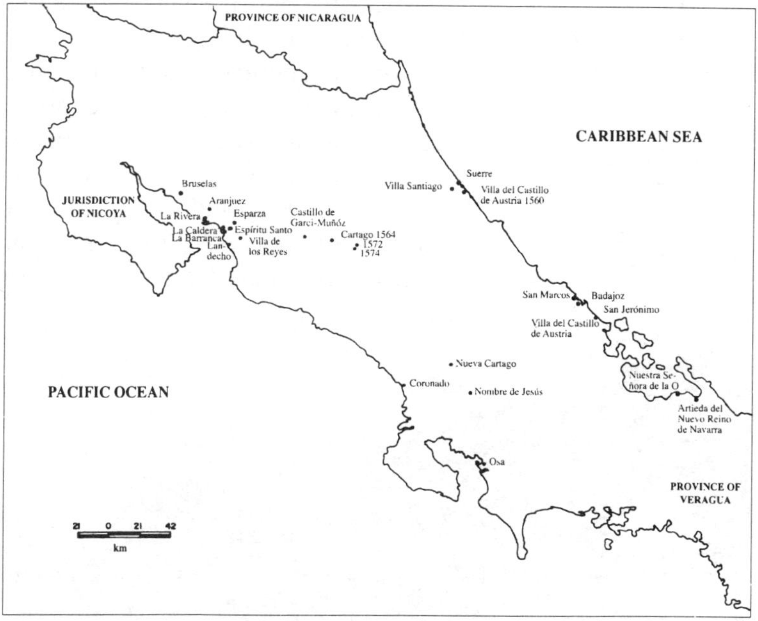

Spanish settlements, 16th century.

The use of persuasive tactics was not entirely successful. In 1564 Vázquez de Coronado faced a series of indigenous uprisings, and in putting them down he ordered the quartering of numerous rebels. The agitation

The greatest obstacle to the pacification of this province is a chief called Garabito... and he is not satisfied with having sacrificed a soldier taken from the party of Licenciado [Juan de] *Cavallón... Instead he exhorts and even threatens all the others not to show due obedience to Your Majesty or to recognize God the Father. For this I have subjected him to trial: he is condemned to death, and war shall be made upon him as if he had rebelled.*

Juan Vázquez de Coronado, December 1562.

reached its climax in 1568, when Cartago was nearly abandoned, something avoided at the eleventh hour by the arrival of the governor, Perafán de Ribera with food and other help. After quelling the rebellion, the functionary of the Spanish Crown began to distribute *encomiendas* among the conquerors, entitling them to exact labor, services and a variety of products from the defeated indigenous groups.

Spanish control over the Central Valley was consolidated by the end of the sixteenth century. Aside from their technological advantages (the horse, metal and gunpowder), the conquerors took advantage of conflicts among indigenous groups, and co-opted their leaders as often as possible. The Spanish also benefitted from the disease,

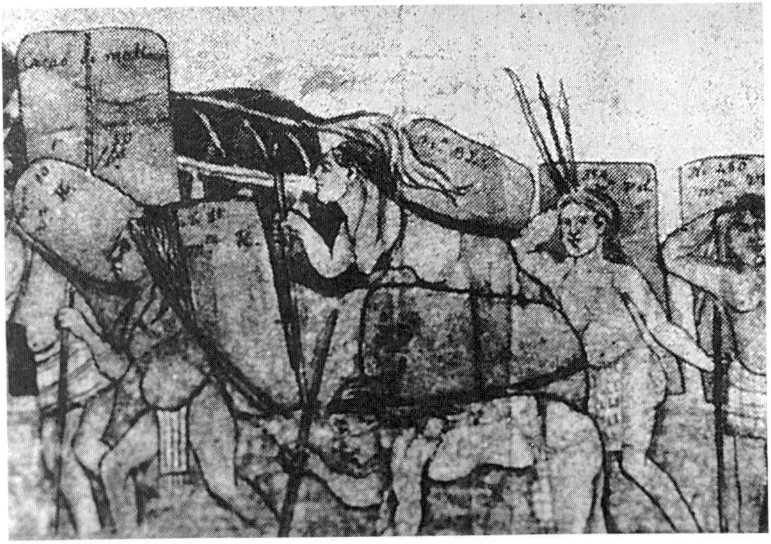

Exploitation of indigenous people.

exploitation and war that they had provoked. Despite this mayhem, the vanquished challenged their new masters militarily on many occasions, although the more common response was to escape to areas where the Spanish could not reach them, in the Caribbean jungles, in the plains of San Carlos and in Talamanca.

Bows and arrows against firearms.

At the beginning of the seventeenth century, Costa Rica was a poor, empty, isolated and marginal colony. For the most part, the territory was either unoccupied or populated by *indios bravos* ("wild Indians"). The principal settlement, situated in the Central Valley, was a tiny world surrounded by mountains, far from the coast and distant from the principal trade routes. The fact that the territory was administratively part of the Kingdom of Guatemala made it easier for the merchants of the north to engage in speculation at the expense of the Spanish settlers of Cartago and their offspring. These new Costa Rican elites on the furthest periphery of the empire were *ultimus inter pares* (last among equals). Not surprisingly, they dreamed of uniting with the dynamic Audiencia of Panama, where the treasures of Peru were unloaded and carried across the isthmus to fleets bound for Spain. The dream, alas, did not come true.

The land is exhausted, and the city of Esparça totally depopulated... The natives perish and [their communities] *disappear... These and many other problems... will cease should Your Majesty order this province joined to your royal audiencia of Panama...*

Council of Cartago, April 1622.

CHAPTER 4

THE EARLY COLONIAL WORLD (1570-1700)

After 1570, Costa Rica participated in the colonial economy through trade in a wide variety of products. Among the foodstuffs that the territory exported were corn, honey, beans, salt, flour, corn biscuits, garlic and chickens. Artisanal products like ceramics, hammocks and blankets were also shipped out of Costa Rica. Primary materials gathered or produced for export included pearls; indigo and dyes made from shells; cotton thread; sisal, agave and other fibers for making cord and tackle; lard, beef jerky and livestock.

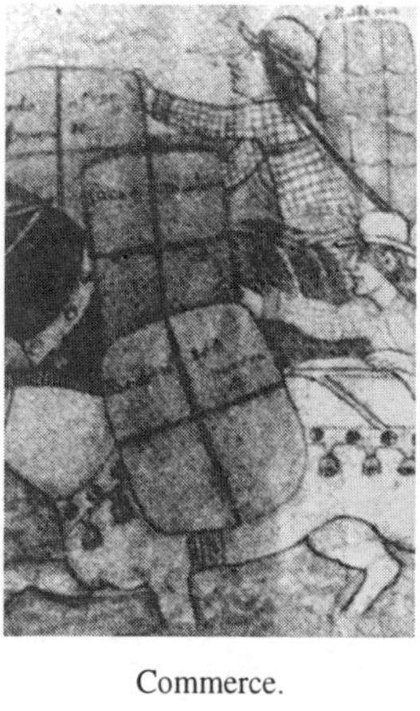

Commerce.

The goods ended up in any number of colonial centers. In Nicaragua, apart from Granada and Leon, they went to the port of El Realejo, the site of important shipyards. In the south, they were destined for Panama, Nombre de Dios, Portobelo, Cartagena and Peru.

Imports were almost exclusively made up of manufactured items: textiles (fabrics and clothes), plates and cutlery, tools and a range of luxury articles. The principal overland route of trade and communication was the famous "camino real", opened in 1601: the road traversed the arduous terrain between Nicaragua and Cartago, passing through Guanacaste and Esparza.

I also inform Your Majesty that together with a city of this province, a port has been founded which apparently is frequented by frigates which come from Panama for corn and honey and oils and sarsaparilla, and birds and wood, and horses and mules are shipped, and this place is called Esparza.

Alonso de Cubillo, Treasurer of Costa Rica, March 1580.

Costa Rica had a number of ports. On the Caribbean, the port of Suerre functioned between 1576 and 1636; in the latter year Moín and Matina were made usable for docking and loading ships. On the Pacific coast the port of Caldera was established sometime during the 1570s, as were those of Abangares and Alvarado.

The dry coastal plains of the Pacific north-west had abundant, valuable hardwoods (cedar and pochote). From the sixteenth century onwards, this area had three shipyards: Nandayure in Nicoya, and Juan Solano and La Barranca further south near Esparza. Vessels of all kinds were built and repaired in the yards, which created a demand for skilled labor, foodstuffs, fabrics for sail-making, and fiber for ropes and rigging. The consumption of these items helped to give a certain dynamism to commerce in the early seventeenth century, which was subsequently enhanced by an active mule trade.

Costa Rica's exports went through three basic cycles of expansion and decline in the seventeenth century. The first cycle was the raising of mules for export, which lasted from 1590 to 1680. The beasts of burden were raised in the Pacific plain of the entire Central American region, from Choluteca to Nicoya and Esparza. They were then rested and pastured in different parts of Costa Rica's Central Valley (Barba, Poás and Aserrí), prior to being shipped from Caldera to Panama, where they were put to work carrying cargo across the isthmus. After 1601, this ocean voyage was substituted by caravans that relied on exploiting the labor of the indigenous peoples of Quepos and Boruca.

Competition from other mule-raising areas in Nicaragua and Honduras put a dent in the Costa Rican industry, which switched to the export of lard and leather to Panama after 1650. The new trade was based on the exploitation of free-ranging herds of cattle, the beginnings of a style of ranching based on the use of vast extensions of land that would come to characterize stock-raising in Guanacaste. However, the people of the area sacrificed cattle in excessive numbers, wasting milk and leaving meat to be devoured by vultures or to rot. The unregulated slaughter was so great that it came to

Exporting mules.

They trade with Panama in tallow from the cattle in the valley of Bagaces ... From one cow they get two or three arrobas [about 11.5 kg] *and they sell each one at eight reales in exchange for goods, so that their profit scarcely reaches three pesos, making the cow on the hoof* [potentially] *more valuable; but because they have no one to buy from them, the owners engage in sporadic slaughters with only the purpose of getting the small quantities of tallow they trade.*

Governor Diego de la Haya Fernández, March 1719.

threaten the very existence of these wild herds. The danger of extinction was only averted in the eighteenth century when the opening of the Guatemalan market to cattle on the hoof led the *hacendados* of Guanacaste to manage the livestock more carefully.

The principal export cycle of Costa Rica in the century between 1650 and 1750 was that of cacao. Cultivation of the cocoa bean was stimulated by sale of the product in Nicaragua. The real boom period (1727-1747), however, was a result of the opening of markets

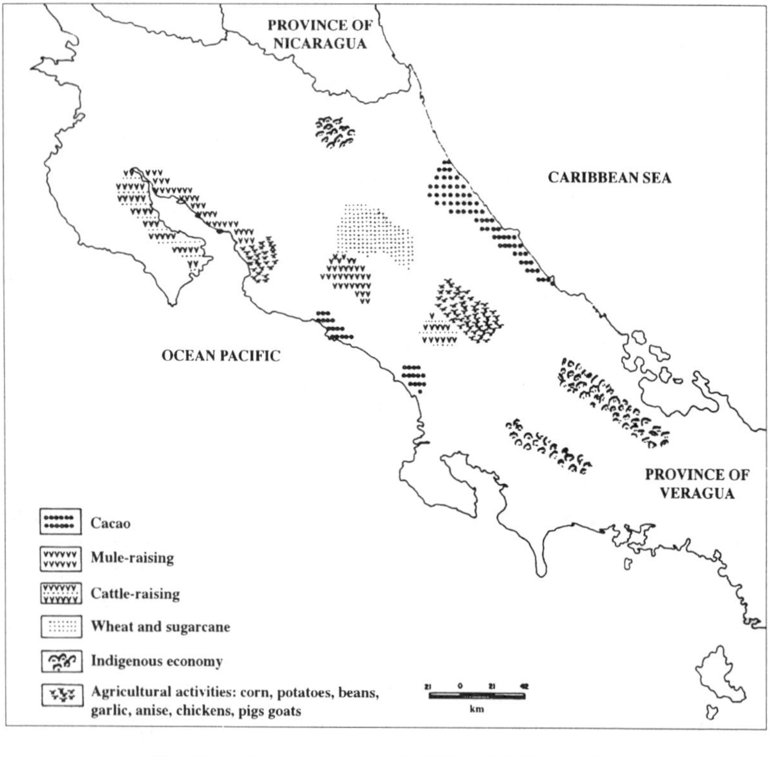

The Costa Rican economy of the 16th and 17th centuries.

for the fruit in the principal centers of the Caribbean: Jamaica, Curaçao, Portobelo and Cartagena. Cocoa cultivation transformed the port of Matina into a center of contraband, especially with the English and the Dutch; it dynamized Costa Rica's colonial economy through trade, and also by giving it a curious monetary unit –the cacao peso (a certain amount of cocoa beans equalled one peso)– established in 1709 in the face of a grave shortage of silver.

The road to Matina.

The hope of securing a continuous, prosperous link with the established flows of colonial commerce was a vain one. The splendor of the cacao boom was fleeting, its rapid decline due to a combination of different factors: taxes imposed by the Crown, an absence of appropriate roads and ports, deficiencies in quality due to production methods, and attacks by pirates and the fearsome *zambos mosquitos* (a Caribbean ethnicity resulting from the union of indigenous people and marooned slaves).

The most important reason for the decline of Costa Rica's cacao boom, however, was competition from other, more potent areas of the colonial world like Caracas, Maracaibo and Guayaquil. Cocoa cultivation continued, and it picked up considerably at the end of the eighteenth century when demand rose in Cartagena, but this boom was even more short-lived than the first, lasting no more than a decade (1770-1780).

These diverse commercial activities were made possible by the exploitation of indigenous and black labor. In 1569, the governor, Perafán de Ribera had formally distributed the right to exploit the indigenous peoples, known as *encomienda:* 85 conquistadors were assigned 208 settlements containing some 22,000 people; at the same time, the Crown was allotted exclusive tribute rights over three towns (Pacaca, Quepo and Chome) containing 2,700 people. *Encomenderos* were obliged to evangelize their subjects; in exchange, they received free labor for their lands and their households, and considerable quantities of corn, beans, fibers, wax, honey, salt and other such products.

I [the governor] *order the said Indians to provide their encomendero... twenty-five hanegas* [1.6 bushels] *of corn... and to give him one hundred and thirteen arrobas of sisal and twelve Peruvian jars of honey, and nine arrobas of wax, and three hundred new blankets... and six arrobas of pita rope... and that they sow for him a field of beans... and that they give him immediately one hundred water jars and one hundred pots... and six Indian men and two Indian women for* [collecting] *firewood, herbage and to grind and serve in his house...*

From the town of Ciruro, made up of 300 indigenous tributaries, for the *encomendero* Matías Palacios, 1569.

As the total numbers of natives declined, the exploitation of the remaining ones intensified, particularly towards the end of the sixteenth century. The constant drop in the potential resources that could be demanded of an ever smaller group of Indians sharpened the conflict between the local representatives of the Crown, those of the Church and the *encomenderos,* since none wished to cede the right to maximize their exploitation of the indigenous people. The results of this intensified exploitation were statistically evident in the 1611 report of a colonial functionary who visited Costa Rica. He calculated that the total number of natives in *encomienda* was a little over 7,000, or 70 percent less than the number distributed in 1569. In the face of this crisis, the Spaniards became more anxious than ever to conquer the areas occupied by the *indios bravos*, the territory of Talamanca in particular.

The efforts to subdue the natives on the Caribbean side, those in the Pacific south and those on the northern plains was a drawn-out process with mixed results. Military expeditions alternated with the attempts of missionaries to pacify areas through the conquest of souls, and with the creation of temporary bases for capturing natives who could be resettled (and so exploited) in zones under Spanish control. The most intense period of such expeditions was the century from 1611 to 1709.

The indigenous groups of these areas offered fierce resistance. Expeditions dropped off after 1709, the year that the *indios bravos* of Talamanca launched a rebellion. In 1710, after the revolt was put down, the Spanish began reprisals with financial and military assistance from Guatemala; the repression culminated with the capture and execution of the leader of the uprising, the *cacique,* Pablo Presbere.

The Spanish had to explore other options for augmenting their labor supply. The principal one was to import black slaves, often in the context of flourishing contraband. The slave

I sentence the said Pablo Presbere... to be... placed on a pack animal and carried through the streets of this city [Cartago]... *and outside its walls, to be tied to a post and blindfolded... whereupon he shall be shot with a cross-bow... and later... his head shall be cut off and placed high upon... that same post...*

Governor Lorenzo Antonio de Granda y Balbín, July 1710.

traffic, closely linked with cacao commerce, was most active in the years between 1690 and 1730. Not coincidentally, 1690 was the year of a major epidemic that decimated the indigenous population in the Central Valley; in its wake, the governor prohibited the labor of natives from Talamanca in the cacao growing areas of Matina, motivating growers to look to the slave markets of the Caribbean.

The execution of Presbere in 1710.

Slaves resisted their lot in a variety of ways, mostly through subtle forms of subverting the master's will rather than through overt opposition. Their labor was exploited fairly cautiously in Costa Rica, given that the elevated cost of a slave made him or her an investment that had to be protected by the owner. Slavery in Cartago and Matina was much less brutal than it was in other colonial areas, those of the Caribbean islands in particular.

The slaves themselves had a variety of opportunities for purchasing their liberty. They might also be manumitted (given their freedom), sometimes a recognition of services written into the will of the master, other times because they were the child of the master, or the mother of his child. At the very least, 430 slaves purchased their freedom or were manumitted between 1648 and 1824. Free blacks and mulattos were particularly visible in the Pacific coastal plain where they often worked as overseers on the vast cattle ranches. Over time, the populace of blacks whose ancestors had come to Costa Rica as slaves were ethnically and socially incorporated through *mestizaje* (racial mixture).

My father-in-law, Seferino Luna... was married to my mother-in-law, Dominga Solano, both of them slaves, and...with their labor they were able to buy their freedom and afterwards they had two free children, one of whom is my wife...

Antonio Calderón, a peasant from Cartago, July 1822.

The beginnings of San José.

In a very agreeable plain ... are situated two hundred and twenty houses with tiled roof and one hundred and ninety-four with straw roof, farms dedicated to milling sugar, others to raising cattle, and others to growing wheat, corn, tobacco, beans, onions, garlic, anise, choreander and dill...

San José, according to Bishop Pedro Agustín Morel of Santa Cruz, September 1752.

The period from 1690 to 1750 saw the definitive decline of encomienda and slavery. The indigenous populace had continued to fall, the *indios bravos* were unconquerable, and the end of the cacao boom also ended the thirst for more labor power. The elites of the era –the principal families of Cartago who traced their lineage to the conquerors– successfully controlled the ranches of Guanacaste and the cacao growing areas of Matina. They monopolized wholesale and retail trade, and they dominated civil, military and ecclesiastical posts. Despite this, they had failed to construct a stable society based on the exploitation of an indigenous or black labor force.

The eighteenth century was a period of increasing racial mixture, marked by the rise of a free peasantry made up of these mestizos and of whites who were the descendants of impoverished *encomenderos.* This peasantry began to populate other parts of the Central Valley, in particular the fertile lands around San José, Heredia and Alajuela.

CHAPTER 5

MERCHANTS AND PEASANTS (1700-1850)

Over the course of the eighteenth century, Costa Rica was transformed by the expansion of peasant agriculture. Population growth around the colonial capital, Cartago, coincided with the exhaustion of possibilities for acquiring land. New generations of peasants had to look elsewhere, and they began the arduous task of settling the western side of the Central Valley. The expansion of the agricultural frontier led to the founding of new towns: Heredia in 1706, San José in 1736 and Alajuela in 1782.

Grinding rice or coffee by hand.

The newly settled areas did not have marked social inequalities at the outset. Still, despite the myth that Costa Rica was a classless Arcadia in the late colonial period, certain differences were visible even among peasant farmers. At the high end were those who owned their own farms; at the low end were those who farmed common lands provisionally made available to them. Some farms had a good deal more livestock than others. These differences in prosperity also determined the capacity of peasant farmers to acquire new technologies.

There shall be a commissioner to regulate the extraction of firewood and other materials from the mountain... and he must ensure that no one person strips or fells more than four trees... Among those who work on the edge of the mountain, each individual shall plant one already living tree at precise intervals of four varas [2.8 feet]...

Dispositions of the peasant owners of the mountain of Candelaria, San José, June 1845.

The basic unit of this agricultural world was the *chácara,* or family farm dedicated to varying combinations of subsistence and commercial agriculture, the raising of cattle, pigs and fowl, and the production of crafts. The larger village community defined how land was to be used, how the forests were to be exploited (for firewood and for building materials), how water resources could be accessed, and so on. Apart from overseeing the commonwealth, village society regulated the everyday life of the peasant families, their values and world-views.

The rural domains contrasted with the town centers of Cartago, San José, Heredia and Alajuela. Although tiny by urban standards, they differed from the rural world because they served as bases of specialized craft production and as sites of the homes of the most powerful and prosperous families. These principal *vecinos* maintained their preeminence in a variety of ways. They occupied civil, ecclesiastical and military positions. They monopolized the circulation of money and they acquired the right to collect the tithe (raking off a percentage in return for the service). They rented parcels of land to poor peasants, maintained large haciendas in Guanacaste and cacao growing areas on the Caribbean, owned slaves and ships, and controlled exports and imports.

Market day in Cartago.

Their wealth came mainly from commerce, which depended on their engaging in unequal exchange with the peasantry. Merchants acquired the surplus (what was left over after subsistence needs were met) from agriculture, from stock-raising or from craft production at less than its potential market value; they then exported it, usually to Nicaragua or to Panama. With the proceeds from their sales on these distant markets Costa Rica's merchants purchased manufactured goods, which they then imported and sold at inflated prices to the peasants and artisans of the Central Valley.

By the eighteenth century, the merchants lacked the means to systematically extract goods and services on the basis of ethnic difference, or through the use of force. As a result, exploitation in Costa Rica's Central Valley assumed the form of a basic mercantile link between two social groups who, although both juridically free, had different economic statures which allowed the merchant group to "buy low and sell high". This system of unequal exchange was reproduced one step up the ladder, between Costa Rican merchants and their foreign suppliers who were better situated in the hierarchy of colonial commerce.

They propose, then, to subject unhappy Costa Ricans to going... all the way to Guatemala to purchase the materials they need, or at least as far as Leon... to buy the same goods already marked up... The demand [of the Guatemalan merchants to prohibit Costa Rican trade with Panama] *is selfish, unjust, oppressive and unacceptable...*

Complaint of the merchants of the Central Valley, August 1813.

As a result, the merchants of Guatemala, Nicaragua and Panama could fix advantageous terms for their purchase of the goods offered to them by Costa Rican merchants. They could also get away with a significant markup on manufactured wares. The merchants of the Central Valley, however, were not exploited as such. It would be more accurate to say that they were incapable of retaining for themselves all the fruits of their exploitation of the peasantry and the artisans. Still, once he ventured outside the territory, the local merchant was at the mercy of his foreign trading partner, just as inside Costa Rica the farmer or artisan was at the mercy of the local merchant.

Because these merchants had no choice but to meet the prices of their foreign suppliers, imported articles were dear. Prices could not be raised excessively, though, since peasants always had the option not to buy at all. As a result, the largest share of merchants' profits depended on the extremely low price they paid for the produce of the land, or for goods coming from the family workshop. The *chácara* was not overly beholden to the laws of this market. It survived by selling only that portion of produce that was left over after the needs of the household had been satisfied. Since agriculture and crafts relied by and large on family labor, the farm could still make a "profit" from the sale of its surplus, even if the price offered by the merchant was extremely low.

In the eighteenth century a new dynasty was installed on the Spanish throne. The Bourbon monarchy, influenced by the ideas of rational administration in vogue north of the Pyrenees, began a series of reforms intended to stimulate colonial commerce and so, by extension, raise the taxation revenues of the Crown. The economy of Costa Rica's Central Valley was affected by these reforms, which included the creation of a State monopoly over the production and sale of tobacco and alcohol.

The regulated sale of liquor increased. Although this commerce was confined to the local market, it spurred

Trapiche (sugar mill).

the cultivation of sugar cane and the manufacture of *trapiches* (small sugar mills). Tobacco cultivation was stimulated first by market demand in Nicaragua, but production expanded considerably between 1787 and 1792 when the colonial authorities in Guatemala granted Costa Rica the tobacco monopoly for all Central America (it fell off just as quickly once the privilege was eliminated).

Most of the commercial expansion in sugarcane and tobacco cultivation took place on the western side of the Central Valley. This was due to the fact that, in contrast to the peasant farmers around Cartago, those in the new areas of settlement were more prosperous and so could invest in land, in livestock and in new technologies. Between 1750 and 1790, economic and population growth shifted away from the old colonial capital and towards Heredia, San José and Alajuela. San José soon outgrew Heredia and Alajuela, largely because tobacco production was concentrated there, and because its farmers had privileged access to the credit of the new administrative entity established there to oversee the monopoly, the *Factoría de Tabaco*.

In a short period of time ... I have seen a large number of good houses erected [in San José], *and those who inhabit them appear out of nowhere. Every day families arrive from other places ... to establish residence in this* [city], *lured by the fortunes that flow from the* [tobacco] *harvests that are the envy of neighboring areas...*

Mariano Montealegre, Administrator of the Royal Tobacco Monopoly, 1818.

By 1800, the Central Valley already accounted for the overwhelming majority of Costa Rica's population. Of the province's 50,000 people, over 80 percent lived in this series of intramontane basins. Six out of every ten were mestizos. Whites (Spaniards or their ancestors who claimed to have no mixed blood) accounted for 6 to 9 percent. After experiencing a resurgence in the second half of the eighteenth century, indigenous people made up 14 percent of those who dwelled in the province (half of these lived in the plains of San Carlos, Sarapiquí and Talamanca). A small black populace, one percent of the total, was concentrated around Cartago and Matina. *Pardos,* mulattos and *zambos* (mixed race people with some black descent) resided largely in Esparza and Guanacaste, and accounted for 17 percent of the total populace.

The territory as a whole hosted a variety of economic and social struc-

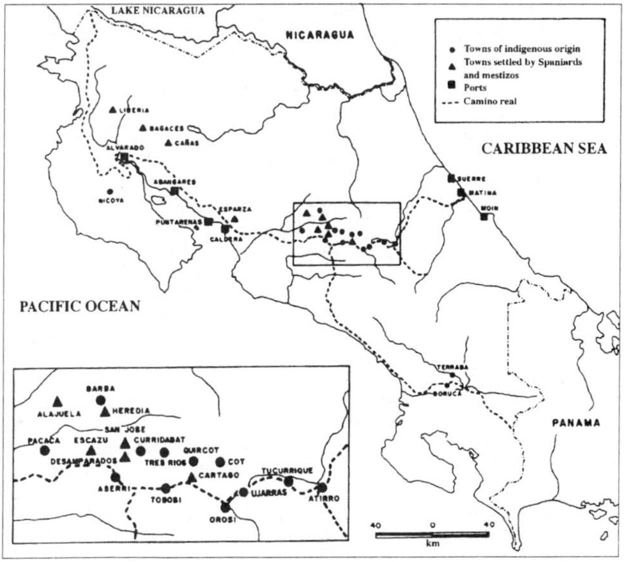

Settlements, ports and roads of Costa Rica, 1750-1821.

tures. Itinerant agriculture was practiced by the indigenous cultures of the outlying regions on the northern plains and in Talamanca. Though in decline by the end of the eighteenth century, the cacao growing areas of the Caribbean coast were characterized by slave labor. In Esparza and Guanacaste a free peasantry, occupied as much in hunting as in horticulture, provided occasional labor for the haciendas. These centers of live-stock raising on the arid Pacific plains benefitted from the expansion of indigo production in Guatemala and El Salvador after 1750, when Europe's industrial revolution stimulated demand for the dye. The displacement of pasturage by indigo plants opened a market for cattle on the hoof,

> *The estate of Don Juan* [José Bonilla, located in Guanacaste] *covered as much ground as a German principality, containing two hundred thousand acres... A small portion of it was cultivated... the rest was a roaming ground for cattle. More than ten thousand animals were wandering over it, almost as wild as the deer...*
>
> John Lloyd Stephens, traveller and diplomat from the United States, 1840.

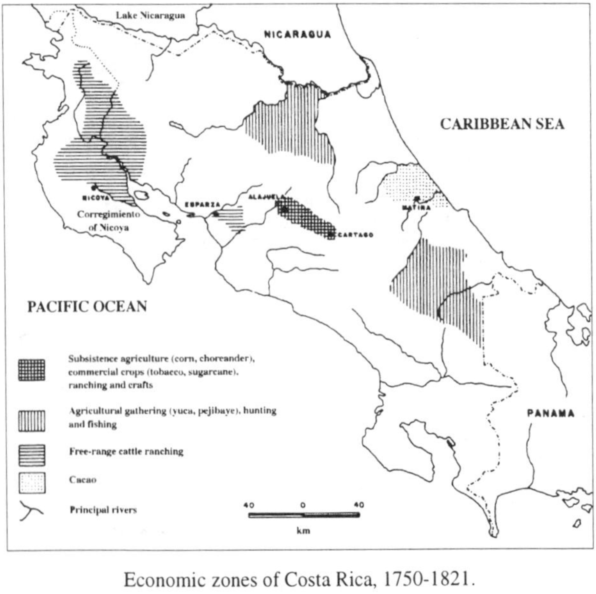

Economic zones of Costa Rica, 1750-1821.

which was raised by the ranchers of the provinces and then driven north.

The Central Valley was economically and socially the most important region of Costa Rica, however. Its economy was based on peasant production, essentially devoid of servitude, and it was an ethnically and culturally integrated area. Mestizos provided the social ballast, and they shared a strong Catholic and Hispanic culture with the elites. True, in the houses of the rich it was common to see icons or the frames of religious paintings made of gold or silver, and occasionally inlaid with precious stones, while in the huts of the poor simple engravings in paper were the norm. But the same saints were worshipped in the household of merchant, artisan and peasant alike, and all held similar beliefs about sin, marriage and death.

Holy Week in San José, 1858.

This world began to change after 1821, when Spanish colonial authority was overthrown in Mexico, and Central America suddenly found itself independent. Free trade, the arrival of foreign entrepreneurs, a small mining boom and the harvesting of Brazil wood all helped to accelerate economic growth. Momentous political and cultural changes followed hard on the heels of these new contacts with the world market.

Mining operations, with their epicenter in Montes de Aguacate, flourished between 1821 and 1843. In 1824, during the first flush of the fever, the *Casa de la Moneda* (the mint) was established in San José. Because it created a demand for labor and supplies from the Central Valley, this mining cycle gave a boost to the internal market as well as helping to monetize an economy that had long suffered from a shortage of metal currency. Nevertheless, the boom was not nearly as lucrative as had been hoped.

Brazil wood, valued for its dye, grew wild in the forests of the Pacific coast of Central America. Between 1800 and 1840, it was an important export product, with the trade reaching its peak in the 1830s. Purchased by English importers in particular, the trees briefly served as a source of capital accumulation for the merchants of the Central Valley. Costa Rica's clusters of Brazil trees, however, were much scarcer than those of Nicaragua. The easily accessible stands were rapidly exhausted, and the surviving trees, situated at ever greater distances from the beaches, were less and less attractive because of the difficulties of harvesting and transporting them.

Having arrived on the coast of Nicoya with the object of loading Brazil wood aboard an English frigate... [I have] *been charged with the clandestine introduction of goods, and for not having paid Docking and Tonnage fees in Puntarenas...*

Fate of the English Captain, Walter Bridge, September 1829.

The desire to find a stable link with the world market was only realized with coffee. The "golden bean" experienced a period of dramatic expansion after 1830, with cultivation initially concentrated almost exclusively in and around San José. The fruit was exported to Chile first, and was then shipped around the Horn and north to the rapidly growing British market. Coffee exports consolidated Costa Rica's foreign commerce: their volume rose from a little over 8,000 quintals in 1840 to almost 100,000 quintals in 1848. Coffee farming, stimulated by cheap and ever more available credit, transformed agriculture into capitalist enterprise, fomenting the privatization of the land and the creation of a market in wage labor.

The merchant families of the late colonial period now converted themselves into the principal *cafetaleros* of the nineteenth century. Their new form of domination was based on a triple control. First, they monopolized credit, especially the annual loans to finance the coffee harvest, but also credit for everyday purchases or long-term investment. Second, they domi-

El Laberinto (The Labyrinth), a coffee estate near San José.

nated the import and the export trade of Costa Rica. Third, they controlled the young industry's principal technology, constructing *beneficios* (processing facilities) that used the superior "wet method" for stripping the fruit of its skin, pulp and husk, and providing the seed –the coffee bean– its basic look and its base flavor. The first *beneficio* was built in 1838 by an immigrant from Catalonia, Buenaventura Espinach. *Beneficios* soon became strategic points of *cafetalero* control over the industry, as well as symbols of that domination.

This early agrarian capitalism in the Central Valley was shaped by peasant agriculture in important ways, however. The actual growing of coffee flourished on family farms, usually ones of less than twenty acres. As a result, the transition to agrarian capitalism in the Central Valley was characterized by strong pressures from below. The balance of social forces which had taken shape across the eighteenth century made it impossible for the new coffee bourgeoisie to violently expropriate the farmers or to submit them to servitude as occurred in the coffee industries of many other countries. The only option left open to the wealthy was to exercise a type of domination that recognized the liberty and the property of their social inferiors.

Non-violent resistance to agrarian capitalism came from some peasant

As soon as the crimson colour assumed by the ripe fruit indicates the time for cropping, numbers of men, women, and children are sent to gather the berry, which is piled in large heaps to soften the pulp for forty-eight hours, and then placed in tanks through which a large stream of water passes, where it is constantly stirred to free it from the outer pulp; after which it is spread out upon a platform, with which every coffee estate is furnished, to dry in the sun; but there still exists an inner husk, which, when perfectly dry, is, in the smaller estates, removed by treading the berry under the feet of oxen; and, in the larger, by water mills, which bruise the berry slightly to break the husk, and afterwards separate it by fanners.

Robert Glasgow Dunlop, Scottish traveller, 1844.

families, often those too poor to be able to invest in coffee production. The rural poor used a variety of legal means to delay the privatization of communal lands. At the same time, the existence of abundant virgin land on the agricultural frontier gave poor or young peasants a chance to pioneer new areas, when land in their birthplace became too expensive due to coffee expansion. This pattern of migration among the lower classes of a small population limited the pool of wage labor available for the coffee harvest, and so coffee pickers had to be attracted through higher wages. This dynamic gave peasants a chance to maintain access to land, and so delayed the emergence of a large landless class of rural laborers.

The same owners of small plots, after finishing their reduced labors, are employed to work on the big haciendas, or find work using their ox carts or mules to transport the berries...

Francisco Solano Astaburuaga, Chilean diplomat, 1857.

Creating an appropriate political system for this newly independent society and this new export economy was not a straightforward matter. On the eve of independence, a fragmented sovereignty was expressed in the various *cabildos,* or town councils of principal merchants and officials. This arrangement reinforced localist identities. So, upon independence in 1821, Costa Rica was not so much a country as it was a territory ruled by four affiliated but rival towns: Cartago, Heredia, San José and Alajuela.

Each town had its own plan for meeting the brave new world. Initially the most obvious course was to adhere to the Mexican Empire, which sent an army to conquer those parts of Central America that did not submit willingly. The cities of San José and Alajuela balked at this, preferring some form of republican independence. As it was, Mexico's imperial dreams collapsed in 1823, while efforts to create a Central American federal republic came to fruition.

Costa Rica participated in this federal experiment for most of the latter's troubled existence (1823-1840), sending funds, assuming a portion of the debt, and electing representatives to the distant assembly. However, the fate of the Central American republic would be decided by events in Guatemala and El Salvador. On the margins of those deep divisions and disputes, Costa Ricans were left to sort out their own internal affairs.

Principal barracks of San José, 1858.

The first order of business was to decide which city would have political preeminence. This produced a great deal of bitter conflict, and a number of battles, inevitably pitting San José against the other three towns (though Alajuela occasionally sided with San José): in the battle of Ochomogo (1823), in the War of the League (1835), and in the conflicts over the controversial leadership of Braulio Carrillo (1838, 1842), bloodshed helped to decide the future of the country.

San José emerged victorious from these twenty years of skirmishing among the major towns. The capital of agrarian capitalism would also be the capital of the State of Costa Rica, and then of the Republic of Costa Rica, proclaimed in 1848 when the project to create a Central American federation had clearly failed. Despite these early conflicts, Costa Rica was fortunate to avoid the prolonged civil wars that set back so many Latin American countries after independence. Of particular importance in this regard, the brief and sporadic battles between the rival towns of the Central Valley did not encourage professionalization of the armed forces. In any case, the country's early economic expansion offered greater opportunities for social ascent than did military prowess, and an abundance of agricultural opportunities also limited the growth of a bureaucratic elite.

Our militia is a collection of honorable citizens: peaceful farmers, artisans and laborers who devote themselves with honesty and constancy to their private occupations, live from their industry and have no aspirations beyond those of fulfilling their domestic obligations and defending the State when the law summons them...

Juan Mora Fernández, Head of State, 1829.

On Sunday the 14th of September cries of 'Long live sacred liberty!', 'Long live our father San José!', 'Long live our lady of Los Angeles!', and 'Long live the united towns!' could be heard everywhere. The exact strength of the people in arms is not easy to calculate; but it can be safely deduced that, counting those armed with clubs, machetes, rifles and rocks, [and including] *women, the number surpassed 5,000. Officers were scarce, and they were barely necessary...*

Chronicle of the popular revolt that overthrew Morazán in September 1842.

The young country had mixed luck in its external affairs. Costa Rica consolidated its sovereignty over Guanacaste in 1824 when the populace of Nicoya decided in favor of annexation to Costa Rica rather than to war-torn Nicaragua. On the southern frontier, however, Bocas del Toro was lost to Colombian expansionism in 1836 (present-day Panama was then part of Colombia). In 1841, the Costa Rican government was capable of a show of strength on the Caribbean side, suspending payment of its annual tribute to the British-backed *zambos mosquitos* (the payment, begun in 1779, was so that they would not attack Matina). In 1850, Costa Rica negotiated its own diocese, thus ending its subordination to the religious jurisdiction of the bishopric of Leon in Nicaragua.

The country's principal diplomatic success was avoiding involvement in the horrendous civil wars that marked the woeful history of the Central American Federal Republic. Costa Rica was affected by the aftermath of those civil wars, however. Following the decisive defeat of federalist forces in Guatemala in 1840, their leader, General Francisco Morazán tried to convert Costa Rica into the political and military base for a new campaign to unite Central America. The attempt ended in September of 1842 with a violent outburst from the plebeians of San José. They overthrew the great *caudi-*

llo with the assistance of disgruntled members of the local elite, and later insisted that Morazán be executed (he was, by firing squad, in the south-west corner of what is now the Central Park of San José).

The leadership of San José was decisive in determining the course of Costa Rica's development, and its pre-eminence was expressed in a buoyant urban culture. By the 1850s coffee wealth had Europeanized consumer tastes in clothing, food and books. It was also behind a diversification of entertainment. One could now attend classes in languages, in dance and in a variety of specialized skills, discuss business over a game of billiards, place bets at the cockfight, and enjoy Shakespeare and operetta at the new Teatro Mora. The city also experienced growth in infrastructure and ser-

Cockfight in San José, 1858.

vices, with the appearance of two-story buildings, street-lamps and pavement, cabs, pharmacies and stores. Later in the century, this bourgeois prosperity and taste would find its maximum expression in the European eclecticism of the National Theater, Costa Rica's temple of civilization and progress, which was inaugurated in 1897 with a performance of Gounod's opera, *Faust* (preceded by the strains of the Costa Rican national anthem and the Marseillaise).

The urbanity of the principal towns, and especially of the capital city, was associated with an expansion of print culture. The first printing press was brought to Costa Rica in 1830, and between that year and 1849 some 17 newspapers and over 100 books and pamphlets were published in the country. Municipal governments sponsored

Teatro Nacional. San José, 1909.

education, though poor towns provided less schooling, and poor families were less likely to send children to school. Nevertheless, the community of readers did broaden and diversify. This process was promoted by the growth of the Casa de Enseñanza de Santo Tomás, opened as a general school in San José in 1814. By the time it was converted into a University in 1843, the works of Adam Smith, Jeremy Bentham and Eugène Sue were circulating through the upper echelons of society.

The *Zapatería Francesa,* a shoeshop in San José, 1858.

Gustavo ad Meinecke, Offers at reasonable prices. The best Wines and Liquors as well as Westphalia Ham, Meats, Patés, Legumes, Dutch Cheeses and Lymbury drinks, Saltfish or fish preserved in oil, Fruits in syrup and cognac, Olives, pickles, Mustard, Sauces and sundries.

Advertisement in the newspaper, *Álbum Semanal*, 24 April 1858.

These new European dispositions of Costa Rica's coffee elite were promoted by the influence of immigrants from the Old World. Costa Rican society experienced an early process of secularization, which was most visible in the behaviors, attitudes and tastes of the wealthy. Merchants and professionals enthusiastically embraced the Enlightenment, Liberalism, Masonry and the ideology of progress (in its capitalist rather than socialist version). In marked contrast to this modernist impulse, peasants and artisans remained faithful to local identities based on village or town traditions, with deep Catholic and colonial roots. This cultural separation underlay a growing social tension, one that became sharper over the second half of the nineteenth century.

CHAPTER 6

COFFEE, CAPITALISM AND THE LIBERAL STATE (1850-1890)

Early in the new year of 1840 an adventurer and diplomat from the United States, John Lloyd Stephens approached San José on muleback. Having recently traversed war-torn Guatemala and El Salvador he was amazed to find social peace, and vast expanses of land planted in regimented rows of coffee trees. The stunning take-off in Costa Rica's coffee industry was stimulated by the high prices that prevailed throughout the nineteenth century, despite short periods of crisis. Cultivation of the "golden bean", initially concentrated around San José, extended to Cartago, Heredia and Alajuela after 1850.

Picking coffee in Tres Ríos, Cartago, 1920.

The colonization of the agricultural frontier carried coffee even further afield. From 1830 onwards, young peasant couples set off to conquer virgin lands. The western portion of the Central Valley (from Alajuela to San Ramón) was the axis of that displacement, and coffee was planted in their pioneering footsteps from 1860 onwards. Thirty years later, coffee flourished in the valleys of the Reventazón and Turrialba, thanks to the completion of the Atlantic Railway. By 1930 coffee was being planted in San Carlos to the north, in Nicoya on the Pacific, and to the south in Tarrazú, though the bulk of the harvest continued to come from San José and environs.

Coffee was an injection of progress into the social and economic life of Costa Rica. Coffee wealth al-

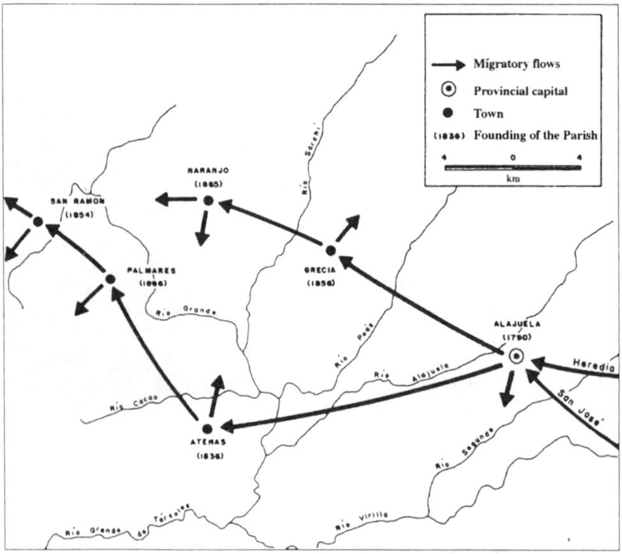

Settlement of the western Central Valley, 1790-1866.

lowed the import of fashionable goods and useful technologies, the opening of new roads and the improvement of old ones (in particular, that which linked San José to the Pacific coast), and the diversification of the internal market. The crop enriched a broad spectrum of small and middling farmers who, on top of a small parcel of land planted in coffee, prospered with the sale of foodstuffs and with the transport of coffee from the Central Valley to Puntarenas, which grew into a bustling port town thanks to the dizzying expansion of the country's international trade.

Carretas (ox carts).

The social and political effects of the coffee boom were visible early on. The losers in this process were poor peasants, hurt by the privatization of common lands, and indigenous communities of the Central Valley, dispossessed of their lands by the feverish pace of agricultural colonization. The only option for the native groups was to move ever further into the wilderness (towards Talamanca, for the most part), a process that condemned them to marginalization, poverty and neglect. The destiny of poor farmers was wage labor. The proportion of agricultural wage laborers in the Economically Active Populace rose from 25 percent in 1864 to 36 percent in 1892, and reached 40 percent in 1927.

[We denounce] *the abuses and excesses committed in the guise of legality against the simple class ... in order to favor with land that belongs to us by legitimate title –title that we have justified with the sweat of our brow– persons associated with the Administration, continuous leeching by the treasury, speculators in the calamities that befall the poor class, and the friends and family of don Juan Rafael Mora who appropriated the largest part without shame.*

Protest of the peasants of Turrúcares, Alajuela, May 1860.

At the apex of the social pyramid, merchants found in coffee an early

Every day one sees businesses fail, distraints, sales of farms at minimal prices, and most people feel the need to cease cultivating [coffee] *because instead of profits it only leaves them with losses.*

José María Castro, President of the Republic, April 1849.

source of stability and wealth that consolidated their power. For those who weathered the economic crisis of 1847-49 brought on by a sharp drop in the international price of coffee, the future looked bright indeed. With its almost 100,000 inhabitants, the society was ever more complex and diverse, but at the same time more integrated and economically dynamic. Agricultural colonization replaced jungles and forests with planted fields and active pastures, while San José lost its village look as it became wealthy enough to dress itself in city finery.

The immediate future, however, was to be tragic. In 1854, in the heat of Nicaragua's civil war, one of the factions sought the help of William Walker, a mercenary (or "filibuster", in the parlance of the time) from the United States. Walker soon took over Nicaragua, and proposed the annexation of all Central America to the southern slave states of the USA. The President of Costa Rica, Juan Rafael Mora (1849-59) appealed to the governments and peoples of Central America to combine forces and drive Walker from the region.

Juan Rafael Mora Porras. Oil on canvas. Tomás Povedano, no date.

Mora supplemented Costa Rica's small regular army with peasant and artisan volunteers, and rode north to meet the enemy. A Costa Rican victory at Santa Rosa, Guanacaste in March of 1856 was followed by the defeat of Walker's main army at Rivas on 11

April. Meanwhile, assistance from the British had allowed the Costa Ricans to seize control of the San Juan River, thus depriving Walker of any reinforcements or supplies. The megalomaniacal adventurer finally surrendered to the Central American armies on 1 May 1857.

The worst of the fighting had fallen to Costa Rica. After the victory at Rivas in 1856, cholera was brought back by the troops and took the lives of almost one-tenth of the populace. This, and the enormous expense of the war, helped to sink the country into economic recession. Between 1856 and 1858 the coffee sector was badly affected by the shortage of laborers

The burning of the Mesón. Oil on canvas. Enrique Echandi, 1896. The horrific representation of Juan Santamaría as a mulatto peasant scandalized fin de siècle Liberals.

We had undertaken our operation to put [the Mesón] *to the torch, when I directed my gaze towards Santamaría and saw that he turned side-ways... and fell to one side, closing his eyes at the same time, I also noted that the burning bits falling from the eaves had lit his hair on fire, I saw the blood flow around his neck and I knew that he was dead.*

Gerónimo Segura, veteran of the National Campaign, August 1891.

Tomás Guardia Gutiérrez. Oil on canvas. A Esttagny, no date.

and the contraction of credit resulting from the war, and the economy did not show signs of recovery until 1859.

Costa Ricans had paid a terrible price to protect their young republic. That heroic sacrifice would come to be symbolized by the figure of Juan Santamaría, a humble laborer from Alajuela whose voluntary act of courage, though resulting in his own death, had turned the tide of the battle of Rivas in favor of the Costa Rican troops. Santamaría was reported to have set fire to an edifice from where Walker's army was decimating Costa Rican troops with rifle fire.

The so-called "National Campaign" of 1856-57 had a bloody epilogue: President Mora was deposed in a coup in 1859, and subsequently shot in 1860 as he tried to return to the country and take power again. Although the execution was exceptional, this was another in a long line of struggles between competing merchant clans who, between 1840 and 1870, intermittently deposed one another through barracks coups in order to gain direct access to the spoils of power. As the country became more complex in every way, such amateur, clannish government was no longer capable of providing coherence and direction to national development.

The transformation of politics began in 1870 under the dictatorship of General Tomás Guardia (1870-1882).

Although authoritarian in character, the two decades of rule by Guardia and his successors, Próspero Fernández (1882-85) and Bernardo Soto (1885-89), saw the expansion of public administration, and the rise of a group of politicians and intellectuals who had a clear plan of reform. Their goal was to create a modern State and society. These men were known as "the Olympians" because of the arrogance they displayed in dictating their Liberal Reforms during the 1880s.

Like similar efforts throughout Latin America at this time, Costa Rica's Reforms were intended to strengthen political authority, favor the expansion of capitalist agriculture, and "civilize" the lower classes. New civil and penal codes were enacted, and police and administrative posts were multiplied throughout the country. The State inaugurated civil registries of births, deaths and marriages. Perhaps of most importance, a centralized, secular, and free system of primary education was created (and made mandatory) to instruct the uncouth artisans, laborers and peasants of the country in new skills and new values.

The great risk [parents] *run of endangering their eternal salvation should they surrender their children to unbelieving male and female teachers, who for that very reason are immoral...*

Warning of the Costa Rican clergy, 1881.

With messianic zeal, the priests of progress –lawyers, physicians, teachers and journalists– began to spread the modern values of patriotism, capitalism, science, hygiene and racial purity. They encouraged their flock to perceive the rhythms of everyday life according to clock and calendar; they preached the control of passions and vices; and they emphasized the bourgeois ideal of the nuclear family as the basis of morality and prosperity.

The Catholic Church cautiously agreed with some elements of this program of reform. But while the Liberals diffused a republican national identity based on the war of 1856-57 and the sacrifice of Santamaría, the Church

Public school in Liberia, Guanacaste, 1909.

promoted the cult of the Virgen de Los Ángeles. Colonial in origin and concentrated in Cartago, this belief acquired a national character after the 1880s. The Church preferred evangelizing to civilizing, and rejected Liberal attacks on its authority, especially over education and the family.

The Church was supported by the majority of Costa Ricans, though the concern of that majority was more than simply religious. The Liberal program meant tighter administrative control, greater privatization of common lands, persecution of alternative (and less expensive) medicine, and the outlawing of some popular customs considered to be "barbarous" (cockfighting, for example). On top of this, by making education mandatory, the Liberal Reform complicated the labor contribution of children to the family economy. The resistance of the laboring classes to the Liberals never reached the point of open rebellion, but it came close.

In the elections of 1889, the Olympian clique tried to maintain itself in power through electoral fraud, after losing to the Church-backed candidate, José Joaquín Rodríguez. Spurred on by the clergy, peasants and artisans took up arms under the banner of the opposition, and surrounded the capital. A civil war was averted only when President Bernardo Soto agreed to a compromise that eventually al-

The call to arms was shouted throughout the neighboring towns... Within three hours... San José was surrounded by some 7,000 men, without counting those of Cartago, where 3,000 were concentrated, or those of Santo Domingo and Heredia, almost 2,000 of whom were making their way towards the latter city.

Account of the uprising of 7 November from the newspaper, *La Prensa Libre*, 13 November 1889.

lowed Rodríguez, the opposition candidate, to assume the presidency.

The events of 7 November 1889 are sometimes referred to as the origin of Costa Rican democracy. That is debatable, to say the least. It is true that, from the 1890s onwards, political parties and periodic elections were crucial pieces in the puzzle of political power. However, the final results of elections were inevitably decided through a combination of systematic fraud, support from the military, and secret transactions. This remained true until after the Civil War of 1948.

Barracks of Alajuela, 1909.

CHAPTER 7

ECONOMIC DIVERSIFICATION AND SOCIAL CONFLICT (1890-1930)

The sale of coffee accounted for nearly 90 percent of the value of the country's exports between 1850 and 1890. This preeminence would be challenged by the banana industry, which was an indirect outgrowth of the coffee economy. Because of the impassable geography that separated the Central Valley from the Caribbean, almost all of Costa Rica's foreign trade went via the Pacific ports. In 1870 the Guardia dictatorship attempted to address this contradiction with the European orientation of the country's economy and culture by contracting two large loans with English banking houses to build the Atlantic Railway.

The railroad in the Central Valley, c. 1873.

The line went unfinished, however, due to technical difficulties, lack of funds and corruption (only one million of the 3.4 million pounds stirling borrowed actually found their way to the railway project). In 1884, the government of Próspero Fernández, short of options, signed a contract with Minor C. Keith in which the young entrepreneur undertook to renegotiate the English debt and finish the railway. In exchange Keith received a 99 year lease on the railway and the port facilities at Limón as well as ownership of vast extensions of the Caribbean lowlands (some 800,000 acres).

It should come as no surprise that the people of Costa Rica, who have no pleasures beyond those that derive from the triumph of peace and the advantages of work and commerce, should perceive with such enthusiasm the first locomotive, pulled by oxen from the Pacific coast, make its entrance into the streets of Alajuela at an altitude of 4,200 feet above sea level. It arrived adorned with flags and accompanied by marching bands, like the conquistadors of bygone days, and it was followed by the multitudes and the preeminent residents of the city until it reached the railway station.

Account from the newspaper, *El Ferrocarril*, 6 April 1872.

Keith's strategy was to finance part of the railway project by growing bananas and exporting them to the United States. The process culminated in Boston in 1899 with his role in founding the United Fruit Company. The Company quickly extended operations throughout the Caribbean basin and established a monopoly over the banana industry, making it the symbol of the economic face of United States imperialism. The military and political dimensions of US power became apparent very suddenly in 1898, when victory in the Spanish-American War left Washington with control over Puerto Rico and Cuba. United States hegemony in the region was cemented by its sponsorship of Panamanian independence from Colombia in 1903. The intervention gave the US exclusive rights over the inter-oceanic canal, which it finished building in 1914.

Costa Rica's national sovereignty had been successfully defended in 1856 but it was showing its limits by the turn of the century. The United Fruit Company controlled the country's Caribbean coast. To the south was the extraordinary US presence in Panama. To the north was Nicaragua, occupied by the Marines from 1912 to 1934. The weight of Washington in the economic and political life of Costa Rica grew increasingly decisive, the dependence intensifying dramatically after each world war (1914-18 and 1939-45).

In order to build the railroad, the various contractors imported thousands of foreign workers between 1870 and 1890. Most of them were Chinese, Italian and Afro-Caribbean

Loading bananas, 1909.

(largely Jamaican). Those who survived the unhealthy and dangerous working conditions and chose to stay on usually became wage laborers in the banana industry or stevedores in the Limón dockyards. The boom also attracted migrant workers from the Central Valley, Guanacaste and Nicaragua.

My mother told me that I were born twelve o'clock Sunday morning. My father was working for the United Fruit Company, and my mother used to bake. She did a lot of things. She was a midwife also, what you call a nurse... My father was a straw boss [a foreman]... *It was in the banana plantations. My father leave Jamaica just like so many others... In those times you just up and down and nobody ask you any questions.*

Joseph Spencer, resident of Cahuita, Limón, February 1976.

That much of the Caribbean coastal plain was an enclave run by a US-based company focussed the budding anti-imperialism of some Costa Rican politicians and intellectuals. This became mixed up with a racist anxiety about the anglophone blacks who made up a majority of the population of Limón province. Meanwhile, especially after 1908, the expansion of banana cultivation was catastrophic for the Bribri natives of Talamanca and Sixaola. The banana zone was the most ethnically complex and politically sensitive region of Costa Rica.

The value of banana exports equalled that of coffee between 1910 and 1920, but the glory years of the industry were those stretching from 1890 to 1914: after the latter year the price paid for the fruit began to decline, rising slightly in the 1920s, only to plunge in 1927. United Fruit's predatory production process was itself largely responsible for this cycle of boom and bust. The profit margins of the company, which operated on an international scale, depended on the exploitation of virgin lands acquired for little or no money. Once the lands were exhausted or invaded by disease, United Fruit simply abandoned them and began cultivation somewhere else. The Company adopted this tactic after 1930, when it moved its operations to the Pacific south region of Costa Rica (with devastating effects on the province of Limón), and the banana industry experienced another round of rapid growth.

The diversification of exports begun with bananas came to include other products of lesser importance whose take-off occurred after 1914. Sugar production, hitherto associated with peasant farming and the simple milling technique of the *trapiche*, now tended to concentrate itself in large capitalist ventures, with the cane processed in a more factory-like mill, or *ingenio*. Cacao production was controlled by United Fruit. Gold and silver was extracted from the mines of Montes del Aguacate and the Guanacastecan cordillera by foreign companies whose most conspicuous shareholder was none other than Minor C. Keith.

Sugar mill in Juan Viñas, Cartago, 1922.

The export of hardwoods was important in Guanacaste. Logging meant the opening of new grazing land at the same time that the sale of wood provided capital to invest in better species of pasture grasses and new breeds of cattle. The growth of cattle ranching in Guanacaste was stimulated by the high price paid for cattle in the Central Valley, where coffee began to displace pastures after the 1840s. Between 1890 and 1930, the privatization of vast extensions of land converted the formerly free-ranging people of the area, whose deep mulatto and indigenous roots combined with an earthy "cowboy" culture, into a poor peasantry with little land and few employment options.

In the valleys of Turrialba and Reventazón, large agricultural estates raising cattle, growing sugarcane or cultivating coffee employed wage laborers who had little access to land. The social makeup of these peripheral areas was markedly different from that of the middle and the west of the Central Valley, where rural life was char-

The Central Park of San José, 1909.

acterized by small and medium-sized family farms that were examples of a more successful peasant colonization of the land.

Starting in 1860, Costa Rica's coffee bourgeoisie had consolidated its control over credit with the creation of Central America's first banks. It now began to diversify its interests by investing in sugar, bananas, cacao, ranching, mining and light industry. Foreign capital, on top of participating in these ventures (and sometimes dominating them), controlled strategic services in the urban areas: electricity, telephones, and trams for example.

Hand-in-hand with capitalist diversification came growing social conflict. On the Caribbean side, workers on the railway line conducted a number of wildcat strikes: the Chinese in 1874, the Jamaicans in 1879 and 1887, and the Italians in 1888. Banana workers struck in 1910, 1911, 1913, 1919 and 1921. Guanacaste was the scene of similar labor action in the mining areas of Abangares and Tilarán in 1906, 1907, 1911, 1919 and 1920. It was also the site of peasant protests against the privatization and concentration of land that peaked between 1920 and 1922.

The large landowners..., in their limitless ambition to monopolize the land, have no compassion, not even for the indigent condition of our families... Since the year 1908 we have witnessed the destruction of large villages that were built up at great cost and with great sacrifices.

Peasants of Quebrada Grande and Guardia, Guanacaste, June 1921.

The violence characteristic of labor conflict in the peripheral areas, which occasionally ended in death, was unusual in the Central Valley where the institutional channeling of conflict had been the norm since the late eighteenth century. However, the period from 1880 to 1930 was marked by a variety of struggles. The poor peasantry and the indigenous peoples made last ditch efforts to defend their communal lands. Small and middling coffee farmers organized to bring ever greater pressure to bear on the processers and exporters to purchase the crop at a better price. And in the urban areas artisans and workers organized and fought to have their salaries increased and their work day reduced.

The Society of Artisans of Costa Rica, c. 1924.

The State cracked down on these popular challenges, but within limits. At the same time, the public power was not averse to intervening in the economic and social life of the country at critical moments, to regulate or arbitrate in labor disputes or to carry out small and localized land reforms. The attention that governments gave to the demands of the lower classes was not a product of accident or generosity of spirit. Following the twelve years of authoritarian government under José Joaquín Rodríguez (1890-1894) and Rafael Iglesias (1894-1902), democracy made further gains. The direct vote was approved in 1913, and in 1925 the secret vote was introduced (for men, that is, since although there was an active suffragist movement in the 1920s, women would not receive the vote until 1949).

Cleto González Víquez on the campaign trail, c. 1927.

Democratic advances coexisted with electoral frauds and secret pacts. But only one coup d'état occurred between 1902 and 1948. In 1917 Federico and Joaquín Tinoco deposed president Alfredo González Flores (1914-17), whose reformist government had established a state bank and introduced direct taxation. The Tinoco dictatorship was overthrown by a civil coalition in 1919. This victory accelerated the decline of the army and the expansion of police forces.

The gradual political integration of peasants, artisans and workers provided the context in which two non-traditional political parties were founded: the Reformist Party (1923), whose leader was the charismatic populist, Jorge Volio; and the Communist Party (1931), led by Manuel Mora. Despite initially suffering systematic persecution, the Communists participated in elections during the 1930s and 1940s. They won seats at the municipal and national level, and they consolidated strong constituencies among urban workers and laborers in the banana zones.

Joaquín García Monge and his wife, Celia Carrillo, c. 1909.

The civilizing mission of the Liberals had a paradoxical result. In 1930 a majority of Costa Rica's 500,000 people could read and write, accepted national values and symbols and participated in election campaigns. But the first three decades of the twentieth century were characterized by the erosion of the ideology of progress. The community of artists, writers, intellectuals and scientists that took shape between 1860 and 1890 had devoted itself to legitimizing the "Republic of Coffee". A new intelligentsia emerged after 1900, whose leading light was the novelist Joaquín García Monge (editor of the internationally respected *Repertorio Americano* from 1919 to 1958). This more radical generation detected a sharp "social question" beyond the glitter of the golden bean: corrupt, greedy capitalists, and exploited and impoverished workers who had to be redeemed through an appropriate education.

The link between these young intellectuals and the artisans and workers of the urban world helped to radicalize working-class culture. During the period 1890-1930, the axis of industry was the shop more than the factory. Although these craftsmen worked for wages, their skill –as shoemakers, cabinetmakers, tailors, typesetters, bakers, masons– was essential to production, and they had a face-to-

Large shoeshop, 1909.

face relationship with their bosses. Anarchist and socialist ideas circulated through this distinct working-class culture, with its own clubs, associations, unions and newspapers. May Day was celebrated for the first time in 1913, and in February 1920 workers organized a co-ordinated series of strikes in favor of the eight hour day, which was the culmination of labor militancy during this era.

The Church, the Liberal State, and the radical intelligentsia all shared an obsession to evangelize, civilize and redeem the lower classes. The source of this desire was a profound rejection of popular culture, whose irreverent style and plebeian concerns worried priests, good bourgeois citizens, and progressive intellectuals alike. Their attempts to transform the behavior, the language and the world views of the plebs, particularly through education, were resisted and manipulated by peasants, artisans and workers, who appropriated what they wanted to, discarding or adapting "decent" culture as they saw fit.

I accustom myself to bathing once a day. Why? The day that I do not bathe, even for good reason, is a day I spend feeling sad, ill-tempered and without desire to work.

Solón Núñez, *My Hygiene Catechism*, 1926.

After 1880 the State published thousands of agricultural, scientific, historical and hygiene pamphlets for distribution among peasants and artisans. Readers in the lower classes availed themselves of this refined literature, while they simultaneously devoured the press of the period (notable for its yellow tendencies), entertained themselves with adventure or romance novels, and occasionally instructed themselves with writings of an anarchist or socialist bent.

The rise of mass culture further complicated the civilizing mission of those at the upper end of the social hierarchy. The theater had contributed to the kind of secularization of culture desired by the Liberals, but after 1914 it was displaced by the rapid expansion of the movies. By 1930 the country had experienced the successful debut and subsequent spread of radio.

Although occasionally surprising, the local contributions to mass culture were essentially limited. The principal products were football (soccer), which flourished in the working-class culture of the cities. While still largely amateur in nature the sport began to be transformed into mass entertainment during the 1920s. Popular music was dominated by the marimba and the guitar in the cantinas, and by outdoor band concerts in the city plazas. This latter activity diversified after 1920, with the forming of groups and orchestras and the opening of dance halls and the country's first recording studios (a number of songs by Ricardo Mora became Latin American hits during the 1940s). The local newsreel appeared at least as early as 1910 when Amando Céspedes began to project his own version of "Pathé" in the country's first cinemas. And in

The wedding went ahead; I put the ring on my wife's finger and the mass ended... We left the church and headed for the Workers Center where we gathered with our family and friends for cake, coffee and lively dancing to the delightful tunes played by the Lubín Barahona Orchestra.

Juan Rafael Morales, shoemaker and union leader, recalling the day he married in 1937.

November 1930 the first Costa Rican feature film, *El Retorno*, was screened at the Variedades theater.

San José is among the most enchanting of Central American cities. Its women are the most lovely of the five republics, and its society one of the most European and North American in style.

The great modernist poet, Rubén Darío, 1891.

Turn-of-the-century San José was dubbed a "metropolis in miniature" by one visitor from the United States. The description was not without foundation. The capital impressed foreigners with its national institutions (the Archive, the Library, the Museum, the Theater), its primary and secondary schools, its parks, alamedas and statues, its stores and bookshops, its Bohemian life, its growing number of newspapers and its diverse and active cultural milieu.

The center of San José witnessed impressive theatrical and dance performances (Ana Pavlova danced in the Teatro Nacional in 1917), and memorable interpretations of classical music (between 1894 and 1929 six symphony orchestras were formed and the great

Librería Española bookstore, 1909.

Costa Rican tenor, Melico Salazar triumphed abroad). This was the pride of a Europeanized bourgeoisie and a stratum of scientists and other intellectuals (some of them radical).

Public space, however, was disputed by a varied group of artisans and workers, and by a sub-culture of paupers, prostitutes and criminals (known during the era as "apaches"). The most plebeian and irreverent dimension of this urban popular culture was centered around the billiard hall and the cantina. It expressed itself in a special slang, in aggressive drinking styles and in the use of drugs.

The Paperboy. Oil on canvas. Rigoberto Moya, 1929.

Opium and marijuana, whose use was not yet clearly illegal, had been consumed by a significant number of Costa Ricans since the end of the nineteenth century. The use of narcotics grew with the new century due to the expansion of medical prescriptions and pharmacies. Addiction to morphine was not unusual in certain upper crust circles, but in 1929 San José was shaken by a moral panic when it was discovered that hundreds of young artisans and workers were consuming heroin. Because of lax import-export controls, Costa Rica was also an important bridge in the international traffic in opium during the early decades of this century.

That's something that everyone knows [the identity of the heroin dealers] *and it's only us, those who don't have money to defend ourselves, it's only us who suffer persecution and arrest, while those who are trafficking are given every opportunity to defend themselves.*

A San José shoemaker and heroin user under police questioning, 1933.

Two men dominated the presidency over the first four decades of this century: Cleto González Víquez

(1906-10 and 1928-32) and Ricardo Jiménez (1910-14, 1924-28 and 1932-36). Despite the European charms of San José, the Costa Rica of "don Cleto" and "don Ricardo" was built on a fragile base. The economy remained dependent on the fortunes of one or two products, and growth was predicated on the parallel incorporation of more land and more labor, rather than on technological change. Social mobility was extremely limited and the abyss between the elites and the middle and lower classes tended to grow, something manifest in Mario Sancho's bitterly critical essay, *Costa Rica: The Switzerland of Central America* (1935), and in the Census of 1927. Starting in the latter year, a drop in the price of Costa Rica's principal export products was the prelude to a terrible economic collapse.

Ricardo Jiménez Oreamuno and Cleto González Víquez, Costa Rica's "Olympian princes", no dates.

CHAPTER 8

THE DEPRESSION, SOCIAL REFORM AND CIVIL WAR (1930-1950)

Costa Rica's Liberal Republic was built on the belief that, given free rein, a capitalist economy based on agricultural exports would lead to civilization and prosperity for all. That certainty evaporated with the New York stock market crash of 1929 and the subsequent global economic collapse. In discrediting free-market dogma, the great slump paved the way for the triumph of a new philosophy based on growing State intervention.

The Naranjo-Zarcero highway under construction, Alajuela province, 1938.

The Costa Rican economic collapse was sharp indeed. Between 1929 and 1932, the value of exports fell from 18 to 8 million dollars, and that of imports dropped from 20 to 5 million. The crisis of the export sector also led to a drastic decrease in the customs revenues that were vital to

State finances, resulting in an acute deficit from 1929 to 1936. Farming families were sheltered from the worst effects of the Depression, but all salaried workers were hit hard.

I arrived at the finca called «El Bosque» [The Jungle] *and I found that the workers were still unhappy about the miserable salaries and the awful way they had to earn them; and that they had sent a petition to the Manager of the Company, and another to the President of the Republic, outlining their hardships and the dangerous lives they led; neither of the two... had sent them a single word in reply and so I told them that the only road left was to begin a general strike.*

Banana worker and Communist organizer, Carlos Luis Fallas Sibaja, October 1934.

The strongest popular reaction against this situation came from the young Communist Party's most loyal constituencies: urban workers, and laborers in the banana zone. The 1933 march of the unemployed in San José ended in a violent confrontation with police, and in 1934 thousands of banana workers went on strike under Communist leadership, paralyzing United Fruit operations on the Caribbean coast.

To deal with the crisis, government began to intervene more actively in the economy. In 1933 the Institute for the Defense of Coffee was created to regulate relations between farmers and merchants. In 1935 a minimum wage was legislated for agricultural workers, and in 1936 bank reforms were undertaken to give the State more control over the money supply. Suspension of payments on the foreign debt in 1932 freed resources to pay for the import of essential products, and to increase government spending. The financing of public works, designed to reduce unemployment, more than tripled between 1932 and 1939, and practically defined the presidency of León Cortés (1936-40), dubbed the government of "cement and iron".

Despite the hardships that it imposed on many, the Depression fomented a modest expansion in import-substitution industry. It was also a fertile era for Costa Rican culture. Between 1928 and 1937 annual fine arts exhibitions promoted the rise of a movement in sculpture that sought inspiration in the indigenous past, and whose leading exponents were Juan Manuel Sánchez and Francisco Zúñiga. A school of landscape painting also took shape during this era, concentrating on rural scenes, and with a particular fixation on the adobe house. During the same period, the novel of social conscience reached its peak in works that dwelled on strategies of survival and forms of struggle among workers and peasants. The

Adobe house. Oil on canvas. Fausto Pacheco, no date.

most famous of these is *Mamita Yunai* (1941) by Carlos Luis Fallas, which portrays life in the Caribbean empire of the United Fruit Company.

The economy showed signs of recovery in 1936, as coffee prices stabilized and banana operations expanded on the Pacific lowlands. In 1939, however, the outbreak of World War II put an end to the recovery. The closing of European markets, formerly the destination of 50 percent of Costa Rica's exports, meant a redirection of trade to the United States. Unfortunately the US bought coffee at an inferior price and could not absorb all the shipments of bananas.

Despite declining State revenues, an ambitious program of Social Reform was undertaken by the government of Rafael Ángel Calderón Guardia (1940-44). The University of Costa

Carlos Luis Fallas Sibaja with banana workers, no date.

Rica was created (1940), a Social Security system was established (1941), Social Guarantees were written into the Constitution (1942) and a Labor Code was enacted (1943). Although the real effects of this transformation were limited, Calderón had laid the foundations of the welfare state.

The growing opposition to Calderón had a variety of sources. The merchant elite were hostile to the progressive elements of the reforms. Furthermore, Costa Rica's declaration of war against Nazi Germany (at the behest of the US) hurt the coffee elite of German origin, who had their properties expropriated and had to languish in detention centers. Inflation badly damaged the fleeting prosperity of the middle class. The political tension was aggravated by a patronage machine that favored Calderón's family and friends over other allies whose support had been crucial for his landslide victory in the elections of 1940.

Calderón's actions led to a confrontation in 1941 with his erstwhile sponsor, the ex-president, León Cortés. As his political strength eroded, Calderón sought an alliance with the Communist Party (the first overtures were made in 1942, and the pact was cemented in 1943). The alliance received the blessing of Víctor Manuel Sanabria, the reformist Archbishop of San José. Church leaders had reason to be pleased with Calderón Guardia: in

The reforms being passed have no objective, no relevance, and no opportunity [of succeeding]. *They mean nothing to the people, who are calling to the high heavens for bread, clothes, welfare, freedom. The social reforms have a hollow ring, they are pure poetic claptrap, campaign literature, and –above all– lies.*

Ex-president (on three occasions) Ricardo Jiménez Oreamuno, May 1942.

1940 religious instruction had been reintroduced into the schools.

This political marriage was denounced by the opposition as "Calderocomunismo", but its legitimacy was strengthened by the unusual circumstances of the alliance between the United States and the Soviet Union in the war against fascism that culminated in 1945 with the defeat of Germany and Japan. The Cold War between the US and the USSR that followed World War II, however, made the alliance between Calderón Guardia and Manuel Mora's Communist Party increasingly difficult to justify, given Costa Rica's location in what US politicians liked to call their "back yard".

Nevertheless, the polarization of Costa Rican politics had preceded the Cold War. The victory of Teodoro Picado, the incumbent party's candi-

Manuel Mora, Monseñor Sanabria and Calderón Guardia, 1943.

date in the elections of 1944, was declared fraudulent by the anti-Calderón opposition, deepening the crisis. The economic recovery after 1945 was unable to mollify growing mistrust in the political system, and the explosion of terrorist bombs in the cities became a frequent event.

Picado's administration (1944-48) brought the Social Reforms to an end, split with the Communists and attempted to provide the opposition with guarantees in the new electoral code of 1946. But it was to no avail. The election campaign of 1948 was waged amid extreme polarization. Otilio Ulate, the editor of the *Diario de Costa Rica,* defeated Calderón Guardia's second bid for the presidency. But the Congress, dominated by Calderón supporters, annulled the official results on the first of March. Eleven days later, without waiting for the conclusion of negotiations between Calderón and Ulate to find a peaceful solution, a renegade member of the elite called José Figueres rose up in arms. The Civil War had begun.

The two forces that would emerge victorious from the armed conflict of 1948 had been on the margins of political life prior to that year. The Center for the Study of National Problems was founded in 1940 by young intellectuals and professionals. The Center's leading figures were the lawyer, Rodrigo Facio and the historian,

This is a report of the Strike Committee [of businessmen who had organized a shutdown] *to the Costa Rican citizenry. The Strike remains in effect throughout the territory of the Republic... Only a very few businesses owned by Calderonistas remain open, and they are being placed on a list of enemies of the national cause.*

Bulletin from the «Huelga de Brazos Caídos», July 1947.

Rodrigo Facio Brenes, no date.

Carlos Monge. Its members resented the stranglehold that the coffee oligarchy and United Fruit had on the economy. At the same time they were virulently anti-Communist. Their sympathy for social reform was linked to a fierce critique of the State, which they accused of being corrupt, antiquated, unjust and incompetent.

The agricultural entrepreneur, José Figueres Ferrer had spent two years in Mexican exile (1942-44) after a volatile radio speech attacking Calderón. Upon returning, he continued his criticisms of the government and formed the Democratic Action Party. In 1945 this party merged with the Center for the Study of National Problems to create the Social Democratic Party which threw its support behind León Cortés and then, after the unexpected death of Cortés in March 1946, behind Ulate.

Carlos Monge Alfaro in July 1972, when he declared: *More than simply possible, it is necessary to implant a socialist style regime in Costa Rica.*

The formation of a rebel army, however, long preceded the elections of 1948. During his exile in Mexico, Figueres made contact with the Caribbean Legion, an organization of exiles whose goal was to overthrow the dictators of the region. The return to Costa Rica in 1944 gave Figueres the opportunity to start figuring in the national political scene and to start training irregular troops at his ranch in San Isidro del General.

On 16 December 1947, almost two months prior to the campaign, Figueres signed the "Pacto del Caribe", in which he agreed that, once he was in power, Costa Rica would serve as a base for overthrowing the rest of the tyrants of the region. The accord was sponsored by Juan José Arévalo, the President of Guatemala, and it was from Guatemala, on 13 March 1948,

People in the countryside and in the small towns and villages are reasonably contented with their lot and could not be expected to flock to a revolutionary standard. It is, furthermore, difficult to understand how some of the rich coffee growers can be in favor of revolutionary activity at a time that the coffee crop is very large and prices for it very high.

Hallet Johnson, United States Ambassador to Costa Rica, February, 1947.

Opposition march of women calling for electoral guarantees, August 1947.

that a plane arrived in San Isidro with men and weapons for the rebel army.

The military option was the only one that might permit Figueres and his supporters to take power since their electoral support was insignificant. This explains the intransigent stance they took during the post-electoral negotiations. The annulment of the elections gave them the excuse they needed to act before any possible compromise could be reached between Ulate and Calderón Guardia, and to begin a war in defense of democratic suffrage, which in reality was fought for something much more than the vote.

The armed conflict lasted five weeks (from 12 March to 19 April, 1948), and some 2,000 people died, making this by far the worst outbreak of political violence in Costa Rican history. Figueres' "Army of National

Otilio Ulate campaigning in San Ignacio de Acosta, San José province, January 1948.

Liberation" quickly defeated and dispersed the rinky-dink Costa Rican Army, and prepared to face off against the pro-government militias holding San José (the famous "mariachis"). The foreign diplomatic corps negotiated a cease-fire and a political pact to end the war: the pro-regime forces surrendered in return for a promise that the property and lives of the losers would be respected, the Social Reforms would be kept intact and the Communist Party would not be suppressed.

The corpses had been splashed with gasoline and they burned like torches, curling up as they were consumed by the flames, offering up scenes worthy of Dante. I could appreciate the fear reflected in the pale faces of children and women, who carried large sacks with their belongings in a desperate attempt to rescue what was most necessary and indispensable.

Testimony of a combatant, March 1948.

Figueres quickly broke key parts of the agreement by outlawing the Communist Party, purging the public sector of Calderón supporters, and sending thousands into exile. The victorious leader also failed to fulfill the Pacto del Caribe, refusing to allow Costa Rica to be used as a base to

Combatants in the Civil War, 1948.

launch attacks against neighboring dictators. Neither did he hand over power to Ulate, instead signing an agreement with him on 1 May 1948 that gave Figueres power as the head of a transitional Junta that would last eighteen months.

The most famous decree of the Junta was to abolish the Army, an act that had great symbolic importance and closed off avenues for future militarization. The Junta also nationalized the banks, thus eliminating the control of the coffee bourgeoisie over credit, which was seen as an essential part of a strategy of promoting economic diversification. The Social Reforms were strengthened, the Costa Rican Electrical Company (ICE) was established, and a greater rate of taxation was imposed on United Fruit exports.

A constituent assembly was convened on 8 January 1949 to write a new

Figueres in the Victory Parade, 1948.

constitution for the Second Republic. Dominated by supporters of Ulate, it rejected the constitution prepared by the Junta, and ended up reinventing the old Liberal charter of 1871. The few additions, however, were extremely significant. The power of the Executive was weakened, and the right of women to vote was enshrined, as was that of the black population. The office of the Auditor General was established, as were a code regulating the Civil Service and a charter for autonomous institutions. Finally, the Supreme Electoral Tribunal was created, making future electoral fraud impossible.

Once the mandate of the Junta was up, Figueres permitted Ulate to assume the presidency, and set out with his closest allies to organize the Partido Liberación Nacional (the Party of National Liberation), founded in 1951.

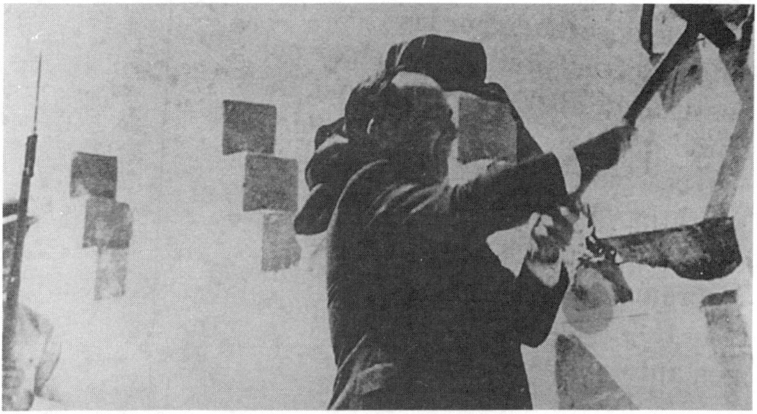

Figueres during the act that abolished the Army, 1948.

I swear that one day, be it tomorrow, be it months from now, when the sun rises over the fatherland, it will light up, to the rejoicing of our nation and of all other nations, the grandiose spectacle of the Second Republic of Costa Rica.

José Figueres Ferrer, May 1944.

In the other countries of Central America, the crisis of 1930 was characterized by the rise of military dictatorships: Ubico in Guatemala (1931-44), Hernández Martínez in El Salvador (1931-44), Carías in Honduras (1933-48) and Somoza in Nicaragua (1936-79). A wave of democratization swept the isthmus between 1944 and 1954, but it dissipated as the polarization of the Cold War breathed new life into another crop of tropical tyrannies supported by the United States. In this context, Costa Rica's political project was exceptional indeed: social justice would be converted into the basis of political democracy.

CHAPTER 9

THE GOLDEN AGE OF THE MIDDLE CLASS (1950-1978)

By 1978 Costa Rica could boast social indicators far better than those of most Third World countries, despite a demographic explosion that increased the population from some 800,000 to almost 2 million between 1950 and 1973. The average Costa Rican could expect to live to the age of 70, infant mortality was a healthy 20 per thousand live births, and 90 per cent of the people were literate. Three-quarters of the labor force were covered by Social Security, and unemployment hovered at a mere 5 per cent.

First day of classes at the University of Costa Rica, March 1971.

This social improvement rested on a spectacular wave of growth, itself the product of the awesome expansion of the global economy after World War II. Between 1944 and 1952, banana exports rose from 3.5 million to

18 million crates annually, and the price of coffee rose from 9 to 68 dollars per quintal between 1940 and 1956. The traditional export sector generated extraordinary profits that were channeled through the State banking system to provide financing for technological improvements and agricultural and industrial diversification.

A plan was initiated to provide credit for coffee and cacao, in the hopes of improving our position in terms of foreign currency reserves by increasing the productivity of our export goods; in 1954 more than four million colones were devoted to the plan, involving not only financing but also technical help from specialized agencies of the Ministry of Agriculture and Industry.

Jorge Rossi, Minister of Finance, May 1955.

Coffee plantations tripled their productivity between 1950 and 1970, thanks to the use of agro-chemicals, something also employed by the banana industry to further enhance their cultivation of disease-resistant varieties of the fruit. Competition was another stimulus to innovation. The State authorized operations by three new foreign banana companies between 1956 and 1965, and facilitated the rise of local banana entrepreneurs who produced an increasing amount of the fruit under contract with the multinationals. In the face of this challenge, the United Fruit Company got into stock-raising, the cultivation of African palm and the manufacture of oil and margarine for the local market.

The income distribution policies of Liberación Nacional increased the spending power of the populace. Greater numbers of consumers provided a basis for the capitalization of other activities, particularly rice and dairy farming. Local consumption also helped somewhat in the take-off in the sugar and beef sectors after 1960. The key to the success of these industries, though (besides access to credit), was the US decision to eliminate the Cuban sugar quota following the revolution of 1959, and the rise of fast foods in the United States.

During the 1950s, the main efforts at diversifying the economy took place in the agricultural sector. The real take-off in industry occurred in 1963 when Costa Rica joined the Central American Common Market. For a decade, industrial growth was vertiginous: over 100 companies were formed in Costa Rica between 1963 and 1975, the majority of them foreign-owned. The weight of tobacco, beverages and food-processing in the make-up of local industry became proportionally smaller as a chemical and

The *zafra* (sugar harvest) in Cañas, Guanacaste province, c. 1975.

metal-mechanical sector expanded. In the process, the workshops of days gone by gave way to the impetuous advance of the factory.

A new public sector nurtured and guided this economic growth, and itself grew and diversified at an incredible rate. The number of state employees tripled to 51,000 between 1950 and 1970, when they made up 10 percent of the work force. In line with a tendency towards a decentralization of power, over 50 new state agencies were created during the same period.

Such intervention [by the State must be]... *undertaken by autonomous Institutions, that is to say, not by the ministries directly, where politics gets in the way, but rather by technical functionaries, independent of the vicissitudes of politics, who are specialists in the field.*

Rodrigo Facio Brenes, 1949.

Public investment manifested itself in schools, colleges, roads, highways, hydroelectric plants, health clinics, hospitals and other infrastructure projects. Neither was the formation of "human capital" (that is to say, people) forgotten. The direction of public ad-

Figueres and Monseñor Odio at the official opening of the Tibás electric plant, San José province, 1956.

ministration was assumed by an expanding group of technicians and professionals, graduates of the University of Costa Rica and foreign centers of higher learning.

Insisting on technical rather than political criteria for the development of the public sector had been a central part of the program espoused by the Center for the Study of National Problems, based to a great extent on the thinking of Rodrigo Facio. Ironically, the putting into practice of this "social engineering" credo, which was supposed to depoliticize the exercise of power, converted public employees into faithful followers of Liberación Nacional. The party used this technocratic thrust to disguise traditional forms of electoral patronage, and to propagate a statist ideology.

One would have to say that the autonomous institutions have served Liberación Nacional, because the party has staffed those institutions with its own supporters and maintained in this way a share of political power even during the periods in which the party has been in opposition.

Mario Echandi, ex-President of Costa Rica (1958-1962), 1975.

In the perspective of Liberación, State financing (using the revenues provided by coffee and bananas) was the key to opening new frontiers of capital accumulation outside the control of the traditional bourgeoisie. The public sector had to put its fiscal resources, its specialists and its infrastructure at the disposal of private capital, in particular that of small and medium-sized business.

The Liberacionista Utopia was a world of cheap credit, endless salary increases, support for co-operatives (the most successful of which were those of coffee growers, who founded

23 between 1963 and 1972), stable public employment, opportunities for social mobility through education, and promotion of the internal market. The partial realization of this dream meant a significant improvement in the living conditions of the populace. The main beneficiaries of the boom were the urban and rural middle classes, who prospered with the growth of the export economy, the expansion of public sector employment, the increase in the size of cities and the expansion of industry. The rise of strong unions of public employees that occurred during the 1960s gave ballast to middle-class prosperity.

Economic expansion combined with social justice not only provided legitimacy to democratic politics, it consolidated the ideological and political leadership of Liberación Nacional. The party also had a great advantage in that the opposition that took shape after 1950 was largely a fragile and incoher-

José Figueres transfers power to Daniel Oduber, 8 May 1974.

ent coalition of all those who had lost out in 1948, essentially made up of the traditional coffee elite and the followers of Calderón Guardia (formerly the bitterest of enemies). Victory by the opposition in the elections of 1958, 1966 and 1978 was only possible because Liberación defeated itself through internal divisions.

The deep conservatism of the opposition became more exaggerated in the context of the Cold War. This made it easier for Liberación to assume the role of a progressive party. Aside from promoting modernization, Liberación governments practiced a more active international diplomacy in defense of the prices of export products, and critical of the United States' support for the dictatorships of the region. This did not stop Costa Rica from supporting the blockade of Cuba and generally acting as a faithful ally of Washington's crusade against communism.

This "golden age" of growth with income redistribution was not without its losers: the peasantry, wage laborers and the environment. Small farmers of grain and other basic foodstuffs, although they often tried to form cooperatives and adopt more modern techniques like the use of agro-chemicals, were displaced by large-scale capitalist agriculture. They were condemned to a future of frustration, poverty, expropriation, exodus and squat-

You have quite a few investments in the dictatorships of America. The aluminum companies take out bauxite almost free of charge. Your... state functionaries and... magnates are treated like royalty... Certain businessmen bribe the ruling dynasties with their millions for the right to hunt on the grounds of their estates. The money is an income tax deduction... Meanwhile, our women are abused and our men are castrated in torture chambers, and our illustrious professors disappear with gloomy regularity... When one of your legislators calls all this «collaboration in the war on communism», 180 million Latin Americans are overwhelmed with the urge to spit.

José Figueres before the Committee on Foreign Relations of the United States Congress, June 1958.

ting. The rise of agri-business accentuated the concentration of land in fewer hands, and subjected the environment to an unprecedented assault. Deforestation was particularly acute in the banana sector, and it also accompanied the growth of extensive cattle ranching in Guanacaste. The massive expansion in the use of agro-chemicals left behind contaminants that remained invisible between 1950 and 1970, and whose full effects are only now becoming apparent.

The persecution of Calderonistas and Communists which began in 1948 lingered on in the years that followed. Although the left maintained its influence among banana workers (the most combative sector of labor from 1950 to 1970), the organizations and the culture of the urban working class tended to disappear. The identity and power-base that they had built after 1890 fell victim to the anti-union offensive of the State and of employers, to urban growth and to a new kind of industrialization. Manual skills which had been essential in the workshop were no longer necessary on the factory assembly line. Industrial growth after 1963 was based on a working class whose members had no links to the labor traditions dating from the turn of the century.

Avanti was the first real factory. Okay, this is where the methods of production changed... At that point the shoemaker stops being a shoemaker, and becomes a shoe worker who puts in eyelets or tongues, or who just does insoles or operates one machine... He's no longer an artisan, he's a piece of machinery, who's not allowed to speak, and who has to be connected to the machine, to the switch.

Juan Rafael Morales, shoemaker, 1987.

Nevertheless, Costa Rica was shaken-up by a variety of social conflicts during the long boom years. Between 1948 and 1954 the protests of urban artisans and workers, and those of banana laborers, were the most significant, as they bravely stood against the persecution of the post-Civil War period. Small and medium-sized coffee farmers mobilized in 1961 seeking to better regulate their relationship with the coffee merchant establishment. During the same period, the discontent of poor peasants began to assume a public form, sometimes through the organization of leagues and committees that had a leftward orientation.

That entire period [from 1948] *up to 1970 was one of violence in the United* [Fruit Company zones]. *The only thing the Company didn't do was shoot us... I had a time when I practically lived in jails... We'd get on the train and the police would be there, we'd get off in some spot and the police would be waiting for us.*

José Meléndez Ibarra, union leader, 1981.

The total number of rural squatter families (*precaristas*) grew from 14,000 in 1963 to 17,421 in 1973, and 2,203 struggles over land flared up between 1963 and 1970, most of them in the Pacific north, the Pacific south and Limón province (areas in which ranches and banana plantations were expanding). The State met this and other similar challenges by creating specialized agencies devoting attention to specific social problems. The desire to deal with popular discontent through legal and peaceful means, which had predominated in the Central Valley since the eighteenth century, culminated almost two hundred years later in a complex and diverse array of institutions.

The objective of these agencies was to brake the momentum of popular mobilizations. To achieve this efficiently, they had to address popular demands to some degree. This dynamic led to different collective actors taking on a corporate character –that is, forming themselves into co-operatives, associations, juntas, unions, boards, leagues, professional societies and the like– in order to more effectively lobby the State.

The unequal distribution of prosperity had a very visible geographical dimension. The urban world (with San José by far the most prominent center)

Domingueando (A Sunday Tour). Oil on canvas.
Tomás Povedano, no date.

concentrated 42 percent of the populace in 1973. It boasted the best services, infrastructure and income, but these advantages came at the expense of the rural areas. The Central Valley, given its political and electoral weight, benefitted in proportionally greater terms from State investment than did Limón, Puntarenas and Guanacaste.

We're from a really poor family. In Turrialba, we picked coffee and made baskets... Dad didn't have stable work... And so we came here, to San José... We came once, but we couldn't make it. We couldn't stick it out, and we went back. And later [in 1963] *we came back again, and we've been here ever since: twenty-some years...*

Driver with an import warehousing firm, c. 1988.

Urbanization was nourished by migration from the rural areas. A century earlier San José had bid farewell to those who set off to colonize the agricultural frontier. Now the city witnessed the return of their descendants. The process was limited outside the capital city, but San José experienced consistent growth. Aside from those who lived in the city proper, 500,000 people visited San José every day in 1976. The majority came from nearby communities, whose civic life dissipated as they became commuter suburbs. Although the growth of slums was still extremely limited as late as 1973, lack of planning meant that urban expansion would become chaotic. San José lost the European charm that had impressed the great poet, Rubén Darío at the turn of the century, and was transformed into an ugly space, lacking in parks and facilities for pedestrians and cyclists, and with an increasingly polluted atmosphere.

Rural culture still prevailed in 1950, but it was inexorably displaced by urban culture in a process linked to mass consumption. The opening of cinemas intensified. There was a notable widening in access to home appliances, especially the radio. The sale of records and comics expanded. And in 1960 television received its Costa Rican debut. Characteristic during this era was the growing penetration of news and entertainment coming from the United States, from the expressions of James Dean to the songs of Elvis Presley.

Locally-produced mass culture was concentrated in certain radio and television programs, particularly variety and game shows, and sportscasts. In the realm of popular music, orchestras like "Lubín Barahona and His Ca-

The Variedades (the oldest theater in Costa Rica), c. 1900.

balleros of Rhythm" began to share the terrain with rock groups. Football acquired a more entrepreneurial face with the construction of stadiums, better salaries for players and managers, and a more defined link with the world of advertising, radio and television.

By and large, the University of Costa Rica was ideologically conservative, and oriented towards training the technicians and professionals demanded by the public sector and Liberación Nacional. Nevertheless, the UCR provided a milieu for experimentation in theater, dance and visual arts (in 1953 Margarita Bertheu held the country's first exhibition of abstract art). The State also supported the arts by creating a series of prizes, awards and cultural agencies. The process culminated in the founding of a

Schiller's *María Estuardo* at the University Theater, September 1975.

Ministry of Culture, Youth and Sports in 1971.

An official culture was institutionalized through State support between 1950 and 1970. There was a notable quantitative increase in literary and artistic production, but much of it lacked originality. The exceptions to this were works created by artists whose formative years preceded 1948: the painters, Francisco Amighetti and Manuel de la Cruz González; the sculptors, Juan Manuel Sánchez and Francisco Zúñiga; and the novelists, Joaquín Gutiérrez and Fabián Dobles. The most significant writers to emerge after 1950 were Jorge Debravo (1938-1967) and Luisa González (1904-), who in 1970 published her short, brilliant and autobiographical novel, *A ras del suelo* (*Dirt Poor*).

That job as an inspector [for Social Security] *allowed him to get a close-up glimpse of a lot of misery... it made him very indignant. For example, in Naranjo* [around 1963] *a leading politician had a coffee beneficio with more than 200 women workers, but he refused to insure them. Among the workers were many single mothers who couldn't take their children to the Social Security hospital and who didn't have money for a doctor. Worse, they were afraid to even give their names to Jorge. They lived in real fear of losing their jobs. Finally he won the confidence of one of them, and she gave him all the names. And that's the way he got them all insured.*

Margarita Salazar, the widow of poet Jorge Debravo, 1974.

The Cold War context determined the cultural climate of the years 1950-70. The cosmopolitanism and intellectual openness characteristic of Costa Rica's urban actors during the Liberal era (1870-1930), were destroyed by the rabid anti-communism of print, radio and television media controlled by a small circle of wealthy families; by the moral conservatism of middle classes bedazzled by prosperity; and by a rebound in Church influence in public life. The ecclesiastical hierarchy distanced itself from the social commitment that had distinguished the Church during the 1940s, and stood against the "option for the poor" endorsed by the Second Vatican Council (1962-65) and the Episcopal Conference of Medellín (1968).

The Costa Rican novel of most prestige outside the country, Carlos Luis Fallas' *Mamita Yunai*, was tacitly prohibited inside the country between 1950 and 1970 because of its revolutionary character. The ideological asphyxia and cultural torpor began to abate after 1967, in the heat of Latin America's guerrilla struggles and the emergence of the student movement throughout the West.

In Costa Rica the origin of student unrest was more cultural than political. It was accompanied by a drug culture in some university circles, and even among high school students (especially those who attended private high schools). But drug consumption was only a small part of a wider process that gave rise to an intellectual vanguard whose typical symbols were blue jeans, beards and long hair.

Costa Rican youth radicalism went beyond love of the Beatles and the Catalan singer, Joan Manuel Serrat. On the 24th of April, 1970 thousands of high school and university students stoned the Legislative Assembly in a protest against mining concessions given to the transnational company, ALCOA.

The cry of "ALCOA NO!" was the beginning of a more profound and

From the death of Sanabria [in 1952] *up until the beginning of the 1980s the Catholic Church in Costa Rica has not undertaken a single initiative in the social and political life of the country. It has, however, consolidated its privileged position to provide religious instruction in public educational establishments, to enjoy financing from the public treasury... to endow itself with costly temples and magnificent rectories, and to be included in every act of State protocol and in the inauguration of public and private works.*

Javier Solís, former priest, 1983.

violent intellectual radicalization than that of the turn of the century. Although the organized left did not know how to take advantage of this, the swing towards radical stances led to a critique of the Costa Rica constructed by Liberación Nacional. Governments tried to defuse the criticism by devoting significantly more resources to health and education. The new left also enriched the cultural life of the country, which witnessed a few golden years between 1970 and 1978.

On June 25th, 1971, at eleven at night [in San José], *I was forced into a jeep without license plates by five men in plain clothes... They took me, like a criminal, to the Second Company, where they proceeded to do an inventory of my belongings... They confiscated photographs... of the riots of June 1st* [resulting from a march

The governments of José Figueres (1970-74) and Daniel Oduber (1974-78) provided a stage where dance, theater and classical music could flourish. The output of publishers and documentary filmmakers also increased. Perhaps of most importance, higher edu-

The 24th of April, 1970 in San José.

cation expanded with the founding of three new public universities: the Universidad Nacional Autónoma, the Instituto Tecnológico (concentrating on technology-related education) and the Universidad Estatal a Distancia (concentrating on extension services). Meanwhile a community of highly-skilled scientists and professionals was consolidated thanks to an active program of scholarships to promote post-graduate studies, especially in the United States and Europe.

The social and cultural splendor of the 1970s was shaken by the sudden rise in the price of oil in 1973, at the same time that the Central American Common Market exhausted its capacity for growth and the price paid for agricultural exports dropped. The full brunt of the crisis, however, was postponed by a rise in the international price of coffee in 1976 and 1977 due to frost damage to the Brazilian crop.

The ephemeral prosperity of the era disguised the actual demise of the dominant economic model. Agricultural diversification, intensified in the 1950s, had provided the revenues to finance industrialization after 1963. Consolidated in the context of the Alliance for Progress, the Costa Rican industrial sector came to be controlled by foreign capital, especially from the US. The industry that arose was technology-intensive and failed to offer abundant employment. Although it

of university students in solidarity with banana workers] *in which some of us were being attacked by the police... The following morning... three of them started to beat me... and they screamed ... «Bust his miserable life. That's how we're going to break these students».*

Alfonso Chase, poet, July 1971.

benefitted from generous tax exemptions to introduce raw materials and machinery, the value of imports for industry outstripped that of industrial exports by 250 million dollars between 1966 and 1972 (not including profits repatriated to foreign investors).

Machinery in the Saprissa Textile Factory, San José, September 1977.

The industrial sector had been converted into an elaborate apparatus for multiplying the value of foreign capital and transferring growing shares of the profits from the agricultural sector out of the country. Given these circumstances, the fiscal deficit sky-rocketed from half a million colones in 1950 to 90 million colones in 1970, and the foreign public debt grew from 29 million to 164 million dollars over the same two decades. State revenues depended on indirect taxes (customs and sales). Incapable of levying appropriate taxes on the wealthy, and unable to police tax evasion, governments chose to accumulate more debt.

The intense decapitalization of the economy provoked by industrialization was exacerbated by a pronounced growth in public spending over the 1970s. Since 1950 the State had dedicated itself to assisting in the accumulation of private capital; it now began to accumulate capital itself. Public investment in productive activities grew at an annual rate of 183 percent between 1974 and 1977.

The so-called "Entrepreneur State", which defined the Oduber government, saw the Costa Rican Development Corporation (CODESA) administering huge sums for public investment in an ambitious program of business creation in industry and agriculture. The result was that the State began to absorb credit that otherwise would have gone to the private sector. This caused important industrialists to shift their allegiance away from Liberación Nacional in the elections of 1978.

Initially the idea was to found a corporation... with the object of developing companies that, due to the magnitude of the investment required, could not be set up by the private sector, in order to get them up and running and then sell them to the private sector. The tendency changed during the government of Oduber. Instead of fomenting small scale businesses, CODESA ... embarked on a disproportionate number of very large ventures.

Walter Kissling, industrialist, November 1979.

The creation of an "Entrepreneur State" also helped to increase the foreign public debt enormously: from 164 million dollars in 1970 it had risen to just over one billion dollars in 1978. At the end of the 1970s the catastrophic costs of the post-war development model became evident with cruel suddenness: growth came screeching to a halt, and then Costa Rica seemed to move backwards in time as the creditors came knocking all at once and Nicaragua, El Salvador and Guatemala exploded in revolution.

Nicaragua celebrates the fall of Somoza, July 1979.

CHAPTER 10

CRISIS, RESTRUCTURING AND ROLLING BACK THE SOCIAL REFORM (1978-1997)

Hit hard by a second oil shock and by a sharp decrease in the international price of coffee, the Costa Rican econ–omy collapsed in 1980. The Gross National Product per capita began to drop in 1979, and fell 11 percent in 1981-82. Real salaries fell a shocking 40 percent over these years. Unemployment rose to 10 percent while inflation ran between 80 and 100 percent annually. In 1984 the crisis was aggravated by regional devastation when United Fruit closed down its operations in the Pacific lowlands.

Workers protest in San José, c. 1981.

The foreign debt reached 3.8 billion dollars in 1984, and between 1983 and 1988 servicing that debt ate up 44 percent of the total value of exports. The State again chose to incur further debt in order to keep the industrial sec-

The representative of the Fund arrived at my office [in January 1981]... *and took out his little sheet of paper, in a personal and private meeting... and he began to say that what was needed here was the suppression of public services... that we have to sacrifice education, popular nutrition... close hospital services... So I said to him: one moment, the only thing that's going to close here are the doors of this country to the likes of you* [because]... *you lack respect... for national sovereignty – so much so that you are going to leave within 48 hours!*

Ex-president Rodrigo Carazo Odio (1978-1982), September 1986.

tor afloat and avoid social chaos. The erratic economic policy of the government of Rodrigo Carazo (1978-82) deepened the crisis. In search of more loans, the administration signed two agreements with the International Monetary Fund, and broke each of them in short order.

The counsel of the IMF was considered suicidal, given the revolutionary Central American context. The recommendations included privatizing state enterprises, reducing public sector employment and social spending, eliminating subsidies on basic foodstuffs, and other measures routinely imposed by the IMF on debtor nations.

The people and government of Costa Rica provided material, logistical and moral support in the fight against Nicaragua's Somoza dictatorship which culminated in 1979 with a Sandinista victory. The move to transform Nicaragua into a socialist country occurred alongside open revolutionary offensives in El Salvador and Guatemala. The widespread warfare shattered regional economic trade and added one more challenge to the crisis facing Costa Rica: dealing with a growing influx of refugees and illegal aliens (300,000 people by 1990).

Despite the severity of the economic crisis, Costa Rica's political system did not collapse. Following his electoral victory in 1982, Liberación Nacional's Luis Alberto Monge had a message for the United States: if Washington wanted to continue insisting that Costa Rica demonstrated that capitalism and democracy could live in fruitful coexistence in Central America, it better start offering up some meaningful relief. The United States Agency for International Development was dispatched to Costa Rica.

USAID was transformed into a parallel Ministry of Finance, making the release of funds conditional upon the Costa Rican government meeting the demands of international financial organizations. Public spending was reduced, as were tariffs on imports (by and large, coming from the United States); State enterprises were privatized, non-traditional exports encouraged, and private banks given a boost (growing in number from 11 to 24 between 1984 and 1996). This foreign entity transferred nearly 530 million dollars to Costa Rica between 1982 and 1984, and understandably garnered powerful allies in business and political circles.

The Reagan administration hoped to convert Costa Rican territory into a southern front in its counter-revolutionary war on Sandinista Nicaragua. Nicaraguan exiles began to operate in San José, sponsored by a US embassy that had seized effective control over Costa Rica's security forces, reorienting them in a paramilitary direction. The local print, radio and television

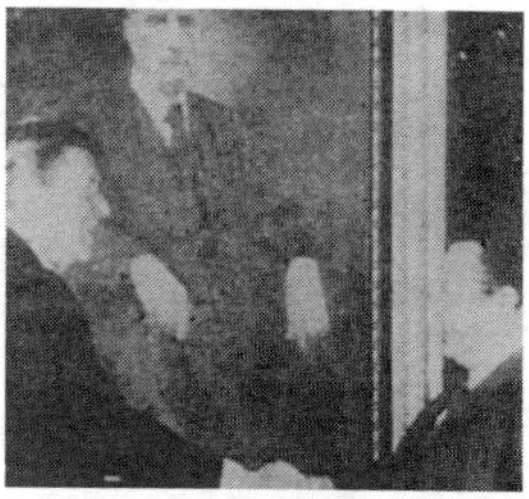

Ronald Reagan and Luis Alberto Monge in San José (behind them, the portrait of Ricardo Jiménez), December 1982.

The monies of the U.S. contributors come to the Costa Rican State [via USAID] *but a mechanism is invented by which they do not actually enter the State coffers, and they remain beyond the grasp of the Legislative Assembly, of the Executive, and of the Auditor General... A series of institutions are created, and nobody knows who they belong to or who controls them... There are subsidies for creating private banks, there are donations, there are low interest rates to promote certain activities, but for the bean farmers there are no subsidies, because that would produce a fiscal deficit.*

John Biehl, Advisor to President Oscar Arias Sánchez, June 1988.

news media revealed themselves to be loyal allies of the US strategy, roundly calling for a militarization of Costa Rica to confront the red menace of Sandinismo, and to crack down on the local perpetrators of a series of terrorist actions that occurred between 1980 and 1983.

The Costa Rican government accepted all but one of Washington's demands: it would not agree to "invite" US troops to establish bases in Costa Rica. The pressure became intolerable, and in 1983 Monge played his last card. He invoked the symbolic weight of Costa Rican history and declared the country's neutrality. He received massive popular support. In 1984 a gigantic march for peace wound its way through the streets of San José, affirm-

Peace march in San José, 15 May 1984.

ing national sovereignty and strengthening the calls for a diplomatic solution to the Central American conflict.

The peace card was the ace in the external policy of the government of Oscar Arias Sánchez (1986-1990). Arias promoted a peace plan that was signed by the five leaders of the isthmus. The Costa Rican initiative intended to undermine US pressure to militarize the country, while reestablishing the regional economy. Arias was able to outmaneuver a US administration obsessed with defeating the Sandinistas militarily, and in 1987 he was awarded the Nobel Peace Prize.

The honor was one of two spectacular Costa Rican interventions on the international stage. The second was much more important for the masses than the Peace Prize (though not necessarily more important than the peace itself): the brilliant performance of the national soccer team in the 1990 World Cup, held in Italy. The team of semi-professional players of working class origin defeated Scotland (1-0) and Sweden (2-1) to advance to the second round. The nation erupted in jubilant celebration.

As the excitement of the Nobel Prize and soccer glory dissipated, Costa Ricans discovered that their country had undergone a profound transformation during the "lost decade". The prolonged economic crisis had provoked dramatic social and eco-

There will be no lasting peace in Central America without democracy... The many problems of injustice, exploitation and misery that confront the region stem from the refusal of the oligarchic groups to cede their privileges... There are people here [in Costa Rica]... *who do not believe in a peaceful solution..., who wish the war to continue regardless of the consequences..., who have never worn out their shoes because they've spent their lives on their knees...: a very intolerant minority of the extreme right who are the ones that... write in the media..., who are the ones who generate those editorials in* La Nación.

President Oscar Arias Sánchez, October 1987.

nomic changes. Two changes were particularly important in the lives of the popular sectors: the rapid expansion of evangelical Protestantism and the rise of Solidarismo, a new form of labor organization.

Juan Cayasso scores Costa Rica's first ever World Cup goal, 11 June 1990.

The Protestant faithful more than tripled in number between 1978 and 1986, from 50 thousand to over 150,000 believers. In 1990, from 10 to 15 percent of Costa Ricans attended evangelical services, at least occasionally. Though the phenomenon is visible throughout the country, it is especially concentrated in San José. The evangelical message, for the most part a conservative one, is propagated by US-based missions whose numbers doubled between 1965 and the end of the 1970s.

Ninety percent of the populace was still nominally Catholic in 1985, but only 15 percent attended mass on a weekly basis. The success of the evangelicals revealed that the Church had been left behind by social and cultural change. Although it tried to deepen its commitment to the poor after 1970, and particularly during the worst years of the economic crisis, its success was limited. This was due in part to the status of Catholicism as the official religion of the State, a condition that ensures ecclesiastical officials receive privileges and subsidies while it co-opts their words and deeds.

Holy Week in Tres Ríos, Cartago, March 1991.

Solidarismo, for its part, is a form of labor organization based on contingency funds saved by workers and owners in individual companies, which provide workers with some benefits and securities while sparing management the negotiating power of unions. First sponsored in 1947 by Alberto Martén, an associate of José Figueres, Solidarismo had a limited period of expansion in the 1950s. Thirty years later, however, in the midst of the economic crisis, it spread rapidly in the private sector, promoted by both business and government. Only 7 percent of worker-management agreements were made by such associations in 1980, but this proportion had risen to 51 percent in 1986. By 1994 the country had 1,694 Solidarista associations and only 600 trade unions. In

The Plan Martén is the great solution for heading off communism... Moscow offers them [the workers] *theories, while with the Plan Martén I offer them money. Let them decide between theories and money: I am certain that if they think, and if they want a future with economic security for their children, they will choose the Solidarity system... The basic reason behind my adoption of the system is that I want to get richer...*

An entrepreneur with extensive coffee interests, 1954.

1996 the movement controlled almost 47 billion colones.

The erosion of trade unions coincided with a profound economic change. For the first time in 150 years the value of coffee and banana exports was overtaken by that of non-traditional exports. Principal among the new crop of exports are textiles, stitched together in final assembly plants (*maquiladoras*) owned by foreigners and highly mobile; pineapple production, an activity controlled by the transnational, Del Monte; ornamental plants; and seafood. The value of these and other similar products rose from 91 million to over 1.1 billion dollars between 1980 and 1995.

The cases of exploitation and abuse of workers continue to grow in the maquila industry... Unscrupulous entrepreneurs [reduce]... *their costs by failing to comply with... obligations, like overtime pay, employer contributions to Social Security and others... In 28 companies... 194 infractions of the labor code were counted ...The majority of infractions involved... a failure to pay the minimum wage ... and demands for illegal shifts of longer than 12 hours... Cases of sexual abuse were detected, as were incidents of the withholding of overtime pay and excessive reductions in the amount of break time...*

La Nación, 31 December 1992.

Diversification meant that the country became less vulnerable to the ups and downs in the price of coffee and bananas. Nevertheless, that advantage was at least partially outweighed by the fall in the international price for virtually all export commodities. Employment in maquiladoras is limited and unstable, and the salaries are poor. Moreover, the success of the industry depends on wide fiscal exemptions that drain the treasury and augment the country's deficit. The most notorious are the Certificates of Tax Deferral (CATs), objects of corrupt practices that have reached scandalous proportions, and have even been used to expedite the laundering of profits from the international drug trade.

The rise of non-traditional exports helped to offset a drastic drop in the price of coffee between 1989 and 1993; in contrast, banana cultivation and ranching increased during these years at the expense of the tropical forest. The rate of deforestation reached 100,000 hectares per year between 1985 and 1988, the highest level in Central America, and one comparable to the destruction of the Amazon region during these same years. An ever weaker State has been incapable of impeding the ecological devastation.

And yet the exceptional biodiversity of Costa Rica is the basis for the promotion of the country as an ideal destination for the eco-tourist. The structure of parks and natural reserves

An earlier style of promoting tourism in Costa Rica (1938).

(covering 33 percent of the national territory) is the fruit of arduous struggles to protect the environment, and it attracts tourists from Europe, Canada and the United States in particular. The rapid growth in foreign tourism began in 1985, and it reached 750 thousand people in 1994. At present, tourism is Costa Rica's principal earner of foreign exchange. Tourism provides a great deal of employment, but the jobs are unstable. Moreover, the industry has expanded at the cost of coastal ecosystems, and much of it is controlled by transnational companies. The first wave of expansion has already come to an end, with annual growth dropping from 21 percent in 1990 to 4 percent in 1995.

The middle classes have also diversified over this period. Prior to 1980, they were made up of professionals, public employees, teachers and small and middling farmers. New middle classes have flowered along with the expansion of the non-traditional export sector, trade, tourism and financial speculation. The possessive individualism of these middle classes, driven by fierce competition, is only outdone by their Darwinian aggressiveness.

We had to put the problem right, and that meant cuts in public spending, an adjustment of tariffs... [taking] *very tough measures... a rise in the sales tax to 13%... a reduction in the number of public sector employees... It was painful for me to dismiss 700 people from the railway...*

President Rafael Ángel Calderón Fournier, March 1991.

Social deterioration is the other face of the latest economic boom. The Structural Adjustment Programs (PAEs), under the direction of the International Monetary Fund, were gently introduced during the 1980s when the country was the capitalist showcase for Central America. This changed abruptly after 1990, with the defeat of the Sandinistas, the pacification of the isthmus, the collapse of the Soviet Union and the crisis of the left throughout the West. The government of Rafael Ángel Calderón Fournier (1990-1994) was the initiator of "shock therapy".

The results have been shocking indeed: deep spending cuts in education and health, and in subsidies to basic foodstuffs. Public employment fell from 17.4 percent of the labor force in 1978 to 14.7 in 1995. The middle class got poorer, the poor fell into indigence and the so-called informal sector (street vendors and other marginal workers) expanded dramatically. Extreme poverty rose almost 50 percent between 1987 and 1991 (in the latter year, 400 thousand people were classified as living in extreme poverty), diseases that had once been eradicated reappeared, and school drop-out rates rose. Real incomes, already in decline, were eroded further by major increases in sales and income taxes.

The imposition of the PAEs took place amid pressures from below that, although decreasing in virulence over time, tended to overflow legal and institutional channels. Typically these protests involved the closing of roads, the occupation of public buildings and

Jesus entrusted to us the loving care of the poor, who in our country represent more than 70% of the total population... As a Pastor I am troubled by the excessive rise in the cost of living, a consequence of taxes that hit the least protected classes of the country hardest. In the name of the poor of my country and with the greatest of respect I entreat the government, when the time comes to raise taxes, to keep in mind the principles of fair taxation according to which those who have the most are those who must pay the most, so that those who have less might pay less.

Román Arrieta, Archbishop of San José, address against the «shock therapy» of the government of Calderón Fournier, August 1990.

other acts of civil disobedience. The main actors in these protests were, on the one hand, residents of urban barrios affected by rate hikes in basic services, or by the deterioration of infrastructure and of public responsibility for its upkeep; and, on the other hand, rural squatters and peasants hurt by the import of basic agricultural products which they had formerly grown for the internal market thanks to government-backed credit and tariffs, both policies that came under attack in the structural adjustment packages. Public employees were the best organized among workers threatened by the PAEs, with unions dating from the 1960s, and they were behind 104 of the 127 work stoppages and strikes experienced in Costa Rica between 1988 and 1993.

[We protest] *the situation of impoverishment and annihilation that we have been suffering for a great many years... a structure of unmanageable costs... taxes and direct charges levied on producers... a total lack of technical help, unjust conditions of production and marketing... all in order to maintain intolerable subsidies and benefits for industrialists.*

Letter sent to President Oscar Arias Sánchez by peasant leaders, September 1986.

Bridge blockaded in Guácimo, Limón province, June 1988.

Social unrest was capable of limiting structural adjustment, but not of stopping it. Neither did it find an electoral expression. The left had destroyed itself in a series of internal conflicts beginning in 1983, and this facilitated the anti-union offensive of the State and business. The period was characterized by a general loss of radicalism among intellectuals and politicians, who now began to ally themselves with their former opponents. Indeed, many who were once prominent members of the left have gone on to play key roles in the cabinets of Rafael Ángel Calderón Fournier (1990-94) and José María Figueres Olsen (1994-98).

The left did not know how to cope with the specificity of our democracy... It died of electoral starvation... Nevertheless... the alternative of the left continues to be valid... While there are right-wing positions, one must continue to be on the left... While there is social injustice, one must... fight for change ... To be on the left is... to be against injustice, to dream of being able to build a better world... What matters now is to keep hope alive and not to allow us to be defeated in the realm of dreams..., dreams of a tomorrow that is better, more just, and freer for everyone...

Manuel Formoso, philosopher, February 1990.

The dismantling of the country's social and cultural vanguards, forged in the political blast furnace of "ALCOA NO!", was linked to the rise of *neoliberalismo* (Latin America's version of ultra-free market conservatism). Liberación Nacional lost its leading role in Costa Rican politics and became the shadow of its traditional opponent, which in 1983 found its definitive modern form in the Party of Social Christian Unity (PUSC). A two-party system was consolidated during the 1980s, though the differences between the two often seem purely formal, leaving citizens without meaningful choice. Figueres Olsen fought the election campaign on the promise of returning to pre-1978 policies, but once in power his government applied "shock therapy" more violent than that of Calderón Fournier, its PUSC predecessor.

The landscape of the Central Valley displays the impact of neoliberalismo on Costa Rican culture. The Central Valley itself now hosts two-thirds of the national populace of 3.5 million. Its political weight keeps other regions from gaining access to a just portion of services and infrastructure. The chaotic kind of urban development stretching from Turrialba in the east to San Ramón in the west is exemplified by the mushrooming of malls, whose fast food areas are the new forum of the post-modern Tico.

The San Pedro Mall under construction in San José, December 1993.

Urban expansion in turn promoted the rise of "transnational culture". The rapid penetration of the "American way of life" was assisted by the introduction of cable television in 1981; by the founding of private schools and high schools that emphasize the teaching of English; by the boom in advertising agencies whose styles are copied from Miami; and by the opening of video arcades and video rental shops. Cinema was one of the victims of this transformation. Between 1980 and 1995, dozens of rural and urban movie houses closed their doors, and in those that remained or were built anew in the malls, screens were monopolized by US distributors (with the important exception of the Sala Garbo).

The privatization of all that was once a basic public service is manifest in the building of medical clinics and private universities (23 of them founded between 1986 and 1995). The number of students attending university rose from 7,192 in 1967 to 79,959 in 1995 – that is, from half a percent of the populace to 2.3 percent. Over half of these are still enrolled in the four public universities, but the motivation to register in private universities is growing greater everyday. The State is itself interested in seeing such a displacement, and has been promoting a model of higher education whereby those of modest means finance their studies with loans (in the public universities a reasonable grant and scholarship system still offers partial support to rural or poor students).

March demanding greater government funding for public universities, San José, September 1991.

The desire to privatize post-secondary education is in keeping with the neoliberal perspective: the financing of culture, and especially of high culture, must depend on the market. One manifestation of that has been the appearance of a market in plastic arts (and especially in painting). Others include the private sponsorship of theater festivals, classical music performances and other artistic activities. A small departure from this trend was the filming of three Costa Rican feature films between 1984 and 1987 (*La Segua, Los Secretos de Isolina* and *Eulalia*).

The transfer of State activities to the private sector is such that, in 1995, the country had only 7,500 national police, while 121 different companies employed 9,089 security guards. These armed men, who can be seen in every commercial parking lot, and throughout the wealthier neighborhoods, are walking examples of the current weakening of public power: apart from relinquishing its monopoly on the legitimate use of violence, the State is incapable of minimally guaranteeing the security of citizens.

The Commission proved that, just like in other countries, Costa Rica is witnessing the penetration of narco-trafficking into State institutions, into banking institutions and into many other public activities, with the object of procuring influence and, where necessary, assistance in the transhipment of drugs or the laundering of money.

Costa Rican Legislative Assembly, Second Report of the Commission on Drug Trafficking, July 1989.

Corruption was limited during the Liberal era, but it widened (and deepened) in line with the growth of the State after 1948. The outbreak of revolutions in Central America between 1978 and 1980 introduced a key variation: the traffic in arms was the prelude to the trafficking of narcotics on a vast scale. The Colombian cartels, in search of safe sites for drug transshipment and opportunities for money laundering, achieved a deep penetration of Costa Rica's political, business and professional groups. US officials calculated that in 1990 a minimum of 12 tons of cocaine were entering the United States via Costa Rica, a volume that rose to 50 tons in 1997.

In a context of social decay, wrought in part by the structural adjustment programs, aggressive youth gangs have flourished during the 1990s. The criminal world has also professionalized itself, in terms of arms, strategies and links with elected officials, executives and lawyers. The influence of organized crime is visible in the creation of networks of female, male and child prostitution (for the most part, servicing tourists), and in the operations of teams specializing in auto theft and drug trafficking. Overflow from the drugs passing through the country has partially created, and certainly satisfied, a growing and differentiated local demand: heroin and cocaine for the better off, crack and marijuana for those of lesser means. The bulk of consumers are young people living in the urban areas, especially in San José.

The neoliberal ethic justifies corruption by defining exchange value as the only legitimate value. The high priests of this world view are among

I've smoked marijuana everywhere, even in the sewers of San José. When we lived in Desamparados, I became a real head. I used to get together with this chick, she was a total operator, but really hot. One time we broke into a house and the police caught us. We were arrested. Now I don't smoke marijuana in the street because the next thing you know you're busted. A few people get together, things start getting a bit crazy and the police arrive.

Construction worker, 1992.

the 15 to 20 percent of the populace that takes home 70 percent of the national income. The richest of these rich use their political, business and family connections to increase their wealth through tax evasion (totalling almost 1.4 billion dollars in 1996), drug trafficking and other forms of contraband, influence peddling, money laundering, patronage, and the embezzling of funds from State banking institutions.

The 1994 collapse of the Banco Anglo Costarricense (the oldest in the country, founded in 1863) is the most notorious example of this new style of super-corruption. That the architects of the fraud that caused this bankruptcy have proved essentially untouchable demonstrates to all the class bias of the

Protest march of employees against the closing of the Banco Anglo Costarricense, San José, 13 September 1994.

Costa Rican justice system. The fate of the 1,700 employees of the institution, who lost more than simply their jobs, offers a stark contrast. The episode was a dramatic symbol of the social and cultural divide that separates the ever more exclusive, prosperous and corrupt elites from the mass of the population who are trapped in a downward spiral of impoverishment.

Costa Ricans' civil rights were buttressed in 1989 by the inauguration of the Sala Cuarta, a special constitutional court, and in 1992 by the creation of an official ombudsman, the Defensoría de los Habitantes. A more important advance during the 1980s and 1990s was the opening of spaces for women in the professions, in business, in politics and in the arts. Currently the most important Costa Rican literary figures are women: the novelist, Tatiana Lobo, the poet and actress, Ana Istarú, and Ana Cristina Rossi, author of *La Loca de Gandoca* (1992), a novel about tourism and environmental damage on the Caribbean coast.

Structural adjustment has had a high social, political and cultural cost. What is more, the rise in non-traditional exports and in tourism has not added up to a model of sustainable development. The country's trade deficit exceeded 650 million dollars in 1995. The foreign debt has dropped somewhat, but in 1995 it was still 3.2

The charges... have not been denied, not by the Costa Rican Tourism Insitute (ICT), not by the Ministry of Natural Resources, Energy and Mines (MIRENEM). They all accept that the damage took place. The problem is that the destruction was made public in 1991... [I had to] *suffer in order to defend my house and the health of my children, I received death threats... Environmental destruction is unstoppable... The environmental policy of the Government* [of Calderón Fournier] *in this moment is a swindle...*

Ana Cristina Rossi, novelist, February 1993.

billion dollars, and in 1996 the internal debt ran between 2.5 and 3.5 billion.

The forced liberalization of trade lies behind these daunting figures, because this has inevitably led to a greater penetration of foreign capital with the subsequent repatriation of profits out of the country. Exacerbating the debt is the government's inability to adequately tax the wealthiest in society or to control their systematic tax evasion. In the face of the debt, political and business leaders argue for the sale of public institutions in order to use the proceeds to pay down the internal debt and make public investment more dynamic. When all is said and done, though, the only thing guaranteed about the sale of the Costa Rican Electrical Company (ICE), the National Insurance Company (INS), the Costa Rican Petroleum Refinery (RECOPE) and other public institutions is that they will be converted into private sources for capital accumulation by local and transnational concerns.

We can trust that justice will be done: 53% of those polled are in disagreement with the statement. Government deputies make laws to enrich themselves: 76% agree. The government robbed the teachers' pensions: 50% agree... Government propaganda is designed to deceive the people: 82% agree. The current policies of the Government are increasing poverty: 84% agree. Campaign promises are a political swindle: 88% agree.

Opinions of Costa Ricans, from the University of Costa Rica's Annual National Poll, September 1996.

The Costa Rica that overcame the Depression of the 1930s added to its constitution a section on "Social Guarantees". That which emerged from the collapse of the 1980s, its political and intellectual leaders lacking in vision, proposes to incorporate into the Magna Carta a section on "Economic Guarantees" for entrepreneurs (and against public spending). The Civil War of 1948 ended with a pact to ensure the preservation of social justice. In 1995, in contrast, Costa Ricans were witness to a quite different accord that significantly undermined the legitimacy of the political system.

President Jose María Figueres Olsen signed an agreement with his predecessor, Rafael Ángel Calderón Fournier, according to which Liberación Nacional and the Unidad Social Cristiana committed themselves to approve a package of reforms that would dismantle the last remnants of the Welfare State built between 1940 and 1978 by Figueres Ferrer and Calderón Guardia – the fathers of the signatories. The civic coalition that mobilized against the pact was defeated after a few weeks of struggle.

Teachers wounded... by kicks in the face... because they protested in defense of their pensions in front of the Presidential Mansion, while a sophisticated spying system directed from... that same mansion... intimidates... politicians and businessmen... Costa Rica is in ruins... Insin-

March against the Figueres-Calderón Pact, San José, 7 August 1995.

cere promises of panaceas are made during election campaigns that are never fulfilled, withering the faith of the citizens in public institutions, while the great challenges facing the Republic are dealt with by means of secret pacts.

Fernando Guier E., lawyer, June 1996.

The epilogue to this confrontation was the violent attack on defenseless citizens by security forces trained by the Chilean secret police.

The negative vision behind the "Figueres-Calderón Pact" is a telling comment on the exhaustion of traditional political parties and ideologies. The current counter-reform also reflects the consensus among a new global elite that the principle of public spending to promote collective improvement and opportunities for social mobility is bad or –as the term "shock therapy" implies– insane. Since modern Costa Rica was built on this principle, its demise is of some concern to a people who are wondering where it might be worthwhile and possible to go from here.

EPILOGUE

THE EXCEPTIONALISM OF COSTA RICA

It would be unfair to end this brief history of Costa Rica on a pessimistic note. On balance, the country's story is cause for optimism. Despite a relatively miserable lot during the colonial era, and although dependent on one or two agricultural exports during the modern period, Costa Ricans were able to build a democratic political system and achieve some measure of social justice in a region where dictatorship and grotesque inequalities have been the sad norm. Between 1950 and 1996, Costa Rica was the only country in all of Latin America that did not experience a breakdown in democracy. These are exceptional triumphs, ones that Costa Ricans are justifiably proud of.

Touring.

In the two years I spent in Costa Rica in the early 1980s... even in relatively remote communities in Guanacaste, I saw that dentists would come periodically to check people's teeth, that children received hot meals... that elderly or disabled people often received pensions, and that even many small producers or jornaleros were insured by the Caja through relatives... I come, of course, from a society that has been severely, probably irreparably, damaged by twelve years of Reagan-Bush free-market madness very much like the model that has been imposed on Costa Rica since the mid-1980s... I... consider it useful to see Costa Rica as a significant experiment and a historical alternative in a world in which there is now...only one economic model, and one that has yet to prove its worth for the great majority.

Marc Edelman, US anthropologist, 1993.

Most of the issues troubling contemporary Costa Rica –a morally bankrupt and rapacious elite, growing poverty and indigence, looming ecological catastrophe, and the loss of control over economic planning– are the effects of "globalization" that, by definition, will seem familiar to readers from anywhere in the world. Messengers of the apocalypse tell us that globalization has stripped the capacity of individual countries to shape their own destinies. If this is true for the large and powerful countries of the world, how much more true must it be for a tiny country on the periphery? Yet Costa Rica's experience confirms that even Third World people make their own history, though they do not make it just as they choose.

Within the small spaces left to them in the design of the grand patterns of the world economy and power politics, Costa Ricans were able to fashion an uncommonly democratic and equitable society. The present challenge is more intense than ever before, the room for maneuver extremely tight, but somehow Costa Ricans must find a way to give democracy and equity new life in a decadent world. If they do not, future chapters on the history of Costa Rica will be unnecessary: the only historical task left will be to determine a date that might best mark the moment when Costa Rica ceased to be at all exceptional.

CHRONOLOGY

Year	Costa Rica	World
12,000-8,000 B.C.	Occupation of present-day Costa Rica by hunters and gatherers.	Paleolithic era.
8,000-4,000 B.C.	Initial settlements and accidental domestication of plants.	Neolithic era.
4,000-1000 B.C.	Transition to the production of foodstuffs.	Bronze age; Ancient Egyptian empire.
1000 B.C.-800 A.D.	Consolidation of agriculture.	Greek and Roman civilizations; early Middle Ages in Europe; Mayan empire in northern Central America and southern Mexico.
800-1500 A.D.	Development of chieftainships (*cacicazgos*), and growing social differentation within indigenous societies.	Feudalism; Renaissance; European overseas expansion; Aztec empire in Valley of Mexico; Incan empire in Andes.
1492		Europeans discover America.
1502	Columbus lands in Cariari (present-day Limón).	

Year	Costa Rica	World
1510-1570	Conquest and demographic catastrophe of indigenous people.	Fall of Tenochtitlán (1521), and founding of Lima (1535).
1564	Founding of Cartago (the colonial capital) by Vázquez de Coronado.	
1569	Distribution of *encomiendas* by Perafán de Ribera.	
1570		Creation of Audiencia of Guatemala.
1590	Beginnings of mule trade.	
1620-1720		Crisis in Europe; decadence of Spain and economic ascent of England and Holland.
1635	Apparition of the Virgin of Los Ángeles, according to the tradition.	
1650	Growth of leather and lard trade with Panama.	
1660	Expansion of cacao cultivation and import of black slaves.	
1702		Bourbon monarchy in Spain.
1706	Founding of Heredia.	
1709	Uprising of the Talamanca indigenous people.	
1710	Execution of the rebel leader, Pablo Presbere.	
1736	Founding of San José.	
1750	Opening of Guatemalan market to livestock.	Expansion of indigo production in north of Central America; High Enlightenment and initial phase of industrialization in Western Europe.
1760	Expansion of tobacco cultivation.	Bourbon Reforms in Spain and Spanish America.

Year	Costa Rica	World
1766		Tobacco monopoly established in Audiencia of Guatemala.
1776		United States revolution for independence.
1781	Royal Tobacco Monopoly established in San José.	
1782	Founding of Alajuela.	
1789		French Revolution.
1808	Riots against tobacco monopoly.	Napoleonic invasion of Spain.
1810		Beginning of Independence movements in Spanish America (1810-1824).
1812	Riots against liquor monopoly.	Constitution of Cadiz.
1814	Founding of the Casa de Enseñanza de Santo Tomás in San José.	
1820	Mining boom in the Montes del Aguacate (1820-1843).	
1821	Independence of Central America (September 15).	Iturbide's Mexican Empire (1821-1823).
1822	Free trade declared.	
1823	Battle of Ochomogo; San José becomes capital of Costa Rica.	
1824	Annexation of Partido de Nicoya to Costa Rica (25 July).	Founding of the Central American Federal Republic.
1830	Introduction of the printing press in Costa Rica; importance of Brazil wood exports.	Francisco Morazán presides over Central American Federal Republic (1830-1840).
1835	War of the League, won by San José.	
1838	Dictatorship of Braulio Carrillo (1838-1842).	
1840	Boom in coffee exports begins.	Morazán defeated by Guate-

Year	Costa Rica	World
		malan rebels; end of the Central American Federal Republic.
1842	Morazán deposes Carrillo and becomes Head of State (April); overthrow and execution of Morazán (September).	
1843	Opening of University of Santo Tomás in San José.	
1848	Declaration of Republic of Costa Rica (30 August).	Marx and Engels publish the *Communist Manifesto.*
1849	Juan Rafael Mora takes power (1849-1859).	
1851		Transport of passengers from east to west coast of the United States via the San Juan river.
1856-1857	National Campaign against William Walker (Battle of Rivas, 11 April 1856; surrender of Walker, 1 May 1857); cholera epidemic kills 8 percent of populace.	
1859	Fall of Juan Rafael Mora; executed in 1860.	
1861		United States Civil War (1861-1865).
1870	Dictatorship of Tomás Guardia (1870-1882); beginning of construction of railroad to Caribbean coast.	Second industrial wave in Europe and the United States; Paris Commune.
1880	Beginning of Liberal Reforms and banana exports. The cult of the Virgen de los Ángeles, promoted by the Church, begins to gain popularity outside of Cartago and to acquire a national character.	
1882	Death penalty abolished.	
1884	Expulsion of Bishop and religious orders; signing of Soto-Keith contract.	
1889	Popular uprising in defense of electoral victory of opposition candidate, José Joaquín Rodríguez (7 November).	

Year	Costa Rica	World
1890	Growing organization of urban artisans and workers.	
1891	Unveiling in Alajuela of statue of Juan Santamaría, hero of the Battle of Rivas.	
1895	Unveiling of National Monument.	
1897	Inauguration of the National Theater with Gounod's *Faust.* Beginning of construction of Pacific Railway (1897-1907); first movies in San José.	Collapse of coffee prices
1899		Founding of United Fruit Company.
1900	Joaquín García Monge publishes *El moto* and *Hijas del campo,* the first Costa Rican novels.	
1903		United States sponsors independence of Panama.
1910	Earthquake destroys Cartago.	Mexican Revolution begins (1910-1920).
1913	Workers begin to celebrate May Day; introduction of the direct vote.	
1914	Reformist government of Alfredo González Flores (1914-1917).	Opening of the Panama Canal; European War (1914-1918).
1917	Tinoco dictatorship (1917-1919).	Bolshevik Revolution in Russia.
1920	Successful strikes for the 8 hour day; influenza pandemic kills over 2,000.	
1923	Founding of Reformist Party.	
1927	Creation of Ministry of Public Health; first Exhibition of Plastic Arts.	Sandino's struggle against United States occupation of Nicaragua (1927-1934).
1929	Panic in San José over consumption of heroin by workers.	Beginning of crisis of world capitalism.
1930	Beginning of economic crisis.	
1931	Founding of Communist Party.	

Year	Costa Rica	World
1932	Founding of National Association of Coffee Producers.	
1933	Founding of Institute for the Defence of Coffee.	
1934	Great strike of banana workers on plantations of United Fruit Company.	
1936	Banking reforms lay ground work for Banco Nacional and Superintendent of Banks.	Popular Front in France and Spain; Spanish Civil War (1936-1939).
1939		Second World War (1939-1945).
1940	Election of Rafael Ángel Calderón Guardia and beginning of Social Reform; founding of the Center for the Study of National Problems.	
1945	Beginning of post-war economic boom.	Beginning of the Cold War (1945-1989).
1948	Civil War won by the Army of National Liberation, under leadership of José Figueres.	
1949	Foundation of the Second Republic; black populace and women enfranchised.	Victory of the Chinese Communists.
1951	Founding of the political party, *Liberación Nacional.*	
1959		Cuban revolution.
1960	Debut of television.	Treaty for Central American Integration.
1961		Kennedy announces Alliance for Progress, the "Marshall Plan for Latin America".
1962	Costa Rica joins Central American Common Market; domination of Costa Rican industry by foreign capital.	
1964		Beginning of military intervention of United States in Vietnam war.

Year	Costa Rica	World
1968		Student-led revolts throughout the West; Prague spring.
1969		The first men on the Moon.
1970	Student protests against concessions to the mining company, ALCOA (24 April).	
1972	Creation of CODESA.	
1973		Oil crisis.
1974	Daniel Oduber elected President; growth of Entrepeneur State.	
1975	Reform of article 98 of the Constitution that had kept the Communist Party illegal since 1949.	
1978	Economic downturn.	
1979		Sandinista Revolution in Nicaragua.
1980	Explosion of economic crisis; growing traffic in arms and drugs.	Deepening of revolutionary wars in El Salvador and Guatemala; Ronald Reagan elected President of the USA (1980-1988).
1983	Founding of the Party of Social Christian Unity (PUSC), and consolidation of two party system; Costa Rica proclaims its neutrality.	Growing intervention of the US in Central American conflicts.
1984	Massive march for peace; crisis of the left-wing parties.	
1986	Founding of the National Center for the Development of Women and the Family.	
1987	President Oscar Arias Sánchez awarded Nobel Peace prize; boom in non-traditional export products.	Signing of Central American Peace Plan.
1989	Sharp drop in international price of coffee (1989-1993); creation of the Sala Cuarta (Constitutional chamber of the Supreme Court).	Fall of the Berlin Wall; end of Communist States in Eastern Europe; United States invades Panama.

Year	Costa Rica	World
1990	National Team wins two matches at World Cup and advances to second round; boom in tourist industry; government of Calderón Fournier begins "shock therapy"; at least 12 tons of cocaine enter the United States via Costa Rica.	Electoral defeat of Sandinistas in Nicaragua; deepening of peace process in El Salvador.
1991	Intensification of the neo-liberal adjustment; massive university protests against the funding cuts of Calderón Fournier government.	Pro-democracy movement crushed in Tiananmen Square, Beijing; collapse of Soviet Union.
1992	Creation of the ombudsman's office.	End of the Reagan-Bush era.
1994	Closing of Banco Anglo Costarricense (founded in 1863), due to massive corruption.	
1995	Political Pact between Figueres Olsen and Calderón Fournier, backed by the leadership of Liberación Nacional and PUSC, to accelerate neoliberal adjustment of Costa Rican society; defeat of the civic coalition against the Pact.	
1996	Acceleration of moves to privatize ICE; private banks begin to open current accounts (an option not available to them since 1948).	Second electoral defeat of Sandinismo in Nicaragua.
1997	INTEL begins operations; at least 50 tons of cocaine enter the United States via Costa Rica.	

BIBLIOGRAPHY

The period prior to the Spanish Conquest is analyzed in detail in two basic works: *Historia antigua de Costa Rica: surgimiento y caracterización de la primera civilización costarricense* (San José: Editorial Universidad de Costa Rica, 1992), by Oscar Fonseca; and *Las sociedades cacicales de Costa Rica (siglo XVI)* (San José: Editorial Universidad de Costa Rica, 1990), by Eugenia Ibarra. The seventeenth century is brilliantly assessed in *La era de la encomienda* (San José: Editorial Universidad de Costa Rica, 1990), by Claudia Quirós.

The legacy of the colonial period, the expansion of coffee and the capitalization of agriculture are themes treated in: *El café y el desarrollo histórico geográfico de Costa Rica,* 3rd ed. (San José: Editorial Costa Rica, 1982), by Carolyn Hall; in *Costa Rica Before Coffee: Society and Economy on the Eve of the Export Boom* (Baton Rouge: Lousiana State University Press, 1986), by Lowell Gudmundson; in "Generations of Settlers: A Study of Rural Households and their Markets on the Costa Rican Frontier, 1850-1935" (Ph.D. diss.,University of California, 1987), by Mario Samper (Westview Press published one version of this work in 1992); in *Historia económica y social de Costa Rica (1750-1950)* (San José: Editorial Porvenir, 1991), by Víctor Hugo Acuña and Iván Molina; and in *Costa Rica (1800-1850). El legado colonial y la génesis del capitalismo* (San José: Editorial Universidad de Costa Rica, 1991), by Iván Molina.

The political dynamics of the period 1870-1950 are dealt with in: *El apogeo de la República liberal en Costa Rica, 1870-1914* (San José: Editorial Universidad de Costa Rica, 1990), by Orlando Salazar; in *Crisis liberal y Estado reformista. Análisis político electoral, 1914-1949* (San José: Editorial Universidad de Costa Rica, 1995), by Jorge Mario Salazar; in *Conflicto y reforma en Costa Rica: 1940-1949* (San José: Editorial Universidad Estatal a Distancia, 1991), by Víctor Hugo Acuña; in *El Estado y la abolición del ejército en Costa Rica, 1914-1949* (San José: Editorial Porvenir, 1990), by Mercedes Muñoz; in "The Origins of Democracy in Costa Rica in Comparative Perspective" (Ph.D. diss., Duke University, 1992), by Fabrice Lehoucq; and in *Fraud, Electoral Reform and Democracy: Costa Rica in Comparative Perspective* (in press), by Fabrice Lehoucq and Iván Molina.

The cultural history of Costa Rica, from 1750 to 1950, is the focus of: *Héroes al gusto y libros de moda. Sociedad y cambio cultural en Costa Rica (1750-1900)* (San José: Plumsock Mesoamerican Studies y Editorial Porvenir, 1992); and *El paso del cometa. Estado, política social y culturas populares en Costa Rica (1800-1950)* (San José: Plumsock Mesoamerican Studies y Editorial Porvenir, 1994), both collections of articles edited by Iván Molina and Steven Palmer. Margarita Rojas y Flora Ovares offer an excellent synthetic vision of literary production in their critical compendium, *100 años de literatura costarricense* (San José: Farben-Norma, 1995). The link between the State and culture since 1948 is discussed in *El punto sobre la i. Políticas culturales en Costa Rica (1948-1990)* (San José: Ministerio de Cultura, Juventud y Deportes, 1995), by Rafael Cuevas.

Social policy before 1950 is analyzed in *The Social Clinic: Moral Policing, Popular Medicine and Heroin Panic in Costa*

Rica, 1900-1940 (in press), by Steven Palmer. Women's history is explored in *Entre silencios y voces. Género e historia en América Central (1750-1990)* (San José: Editorial Porvenir y Centro Nacional para el Desarrollo de la Mujer y la Familia, 1997), edited by Eugenia Rodríguez.

The three best overviews of contemporary Costa Rica (since 1948) are: *Costa Rica: A Geographical Interpretation in Historical Perspective* (Boulder, Colorado: Westview Press, 1985), by Carolyn Hall; and, by Jorge Rovira, *Estado y política económica en Costa Rica, 1948-1970* (San José: Editorial Porvenir, 1982); and *Costa Rica en los años '80* (San José: Editorial Porvenir, 1987).

The connection between the structural adjustment programs (PAEs) and the sharpening of social differentiation is the theme of an important book by José Luis Vega Carballo, *Pobreza y coyuntura social en Costa Rica en la época de los PAEs* (Heredia: CEDAL, 1992). Mary Clark evaluates the growth of non-traditional exports in her thesis, "Transnational Alliances and Development Strategies: The Transition to Export-led Growth in Costa Rica, 1983-1990" (Ph.D. diss., University of Wisconsin, 1993). Popular culture in the era of the PAEs is treated in *Sueños y sudores en la vida cotidiana. Trabajadores y trabajadoras de la maquila y la construcción en Costa Rica* (San José: Editorial Universidad de Costa Rica, 1997), by Carlos Sandoval.

In terms of research on the major regions of Costa Rica, the Caribbean coast and Guanacaste have received superb synthetic treatments in: Philippe Bourgois, *Ethnicity at Work: Divided Labor on a Central American Banana Plantation* (Baltimore: The John Hopkins University Press, 1989); and Marc Edelman, *The Logic of the Latifundio: The Large Estates of Northwestern Costa Rica Since the Late Nineteenth Century* (Stanford: Stanford University Press, 1992).

Those wishing to put the Costa Rican case in its Central American context can read: Héctor Pérez, *A Brief History of Central America* (Los Angeles: University of California Press, 1989); Victor Bulmer Thomas, *The Political Economy of Cen-*

tral America Since 1920 (Cambridge: Cambridge University Press, 1988); and the six volumes of the *Historia General de Centroamérica* (Madrid: Facultad Latinoamericana de Ciencias Sociales-Comisión Quinto Centenario, 1993).

The available bibliography on Costa Rica is abundant and diverse, and the preceding list is intended merely as a guide for the reader interested in expanding their knowledge. The *Revista de Historia,* the *Anuario de Estudios Sociales Centroamericanos* and the *Revista de Ciencias Sociales,* among other periodical publications, contain articles on specific themes that will bring the reader up to date on specialized social science research on Costa Rican issues.

The illustrations in this book come from previously cited works, and from the photographic and art collections of: the Museo Nacional de Costa Rica; the Museo de Arte Costarricense; the Museo Histórico Cultural Juan Santamaría; the Archivo Nacional de Costa Rica; the Patronato Nacional de la Infancia; the Archivo de la Universidad de Costa Rica; the photographic archives of *La Nación;* the pages of the *Semanario Universidad;* and the private collection of Julio Jiménez. The drawings are from the "Álbum de Figueroa", the famous (though as yet unpublished) work composed by José María Figueroa Oreamuno between 1873 and 1883.

ILLUSTRATIONS

ILLUSTRATIONS

INDEX

INDEX

AUTHORS

Steven Palmer was born in Montreal in 1961. He has a Ph.D. in Latin American History from Columbia University in the City of New York (1990), and he has taught at the University of Iowa, Memorial University of Newfoundland, the University of Montreal and the University of Costa Rica. He is the author of a wide variety of studies on Costa Rican history, from the origins of nationalism to the social history of medicine and public health.

Iván Molina was born in Alajuela in 1961. He has a Master's degree in History from the University of Costa Rica (1984), and he has taught at the National University (UNA) in Heredia and at the University of Costa Rica (UCR). He is the author of many

Books by Molina and Palmer have been awarded the Aquileo Echeverría National Prize in History, the Cleto González Víquez Prize in History, and the Ancora Prize of La Nación, *Costa Rica's premier newspaper. Their research has been financed by the University of Costa Rica, the Social Sciences and Humanities Research Council of Canada and the National Endowment for the Humanities (Washington).*

books and articles on Costa Rica history, from the colonial economy to the book trade in the nineteenth and twenty centuries.

This is the fifth book that the authors have collaborated on. They co-wrote *Costa Rica (1930-1996). Historia de una sociedad,* and *La voluntad radiante. Cultura impresa, magia y medicina en Costa Rica (1897-1932).* They also co-edited two collections of articles on Costa Rican cultural history: *Héroes al gusto y libros de moda. Sociedad y cambio cultural en Costa Rica (1750/1900),* and *El paso del cometa. Estado, política social y culturas populares en Costa Rica (1800-1950).*

Questions and comments on this book?
Write to:

Steven Palmer
5 Portugal Cove Rd.
St. John's, NF
Canada A1B 2L5
e-mail:
greateastern@stjohns.cbc.ca

Iván Molina
Escuela de Historia
Universidad de Costa Rica
San José, Costa Rica,
Central America.
e-mail:
ivanm@cariari.ucr.ac.cr

Este libro se terminó de imprimir en la Sección de Impresión del SIEDIN, en el mes de agosto de 2006.

Universidad de Costa Rica
Ciudad Universitaria Rodrigo Facio
San José, Costa Rica, A.C.